The Origin of the Theater

The Origin of the Theater

The Origin of the Theater

An Essay by
BENJAMIN HUNNINGHER

A Dramabook
HILL AND WANG · NEW YORK

Benjamin Hunningher is a distinguished theatre and art critic. He grew up in Amsterdam and received his Ph.D. in literature and history at the University of Utrecht in 1931. For the *Nieuwe Rotterdamse Courant*, one of Europe's leading newspapers, he wrote art and theatre criticism until 1941. After the war, as head of the Drama Department in the Ministry for Education and Arts at The Hague, he organized the National Theatre and its five repertory companies.

Dr. Hunningher is the author of several books on art and the theatre. Among his theatre books are *Theatre and Education* (1946); *Theatre and Realisme* (1947); *Medieval Liturgy and the Theatre* (1954). He has also worked in Greece and written a book on the Dionysian theatre in Athens.

Since 1948 Professor Hunningher has been teaching at Columbia University, where he holds the Queen Wilhelmina Chair, dedicated to the culture of the Low Countries.

Contents

Contents

List of Illustrations

ix

The Origin of the Theater

The Origin of the Theater

1: The Problem

THOUGH THE problems surrounding the dramatic art of our times are many, one of them seems to have been definitely and permanently solved—the problem of origin. That origin lies in the medieval Christian Church; so much is certain and free from disagreement. In itself, this very unanimity of opinion is remarkable, especially when we consider the contradictions involved in such a conclusion. On the one hand stands Christianity jubilant in its freedom from the material world and its participation in eternal invisible salvation; on the other, an art concerned only with what the eye can see and the ear can hear in our painful but glorious mortality.

Both sides have been aware of this contradiction—how many thunderous interdictions has the Church not hurled at the theater down the ages, and how often has an angry and scornful anticlericalism not responded from the stage? And have not Church and stage now drifted so far apart that their original unity must arouse a certain amount of speculation?

One must certainly wonder at Chrysostom's and Tertullian's sharp warnings that the stage causes the destruction of man's character and the doom of his soul.[1] Stage play is deceitful, said Chrysostom in one

1. Chrysostom, *Opera*, ed. Montfaucon, vol. II, p. 318. The polemic writings of these patriarchs is discussed extensively in *Der Mimus* by Hermann Reich, Berlin, 1903, p. 109 seq. (Reich's main thesis was attacked by Philip S. Allen, "The Mediaeval Mimus," *Modern Philology*, VII, p. 327 seq. and VIII, p. 139 seq.) See also the antiquated, but still valuable study by Heinrich Alt, *Theater und Kirche*, Berlin, 1846, p. 310 seq. and Maxim J. Rudwin, *The Origin of the German Carnival Comedy*, New York, 1920.

of his many attacks upon the theater; neither Tertullian nor Cyprian missed an opportunity to stress the stage's misuse of man's capacities, so that a Christian striving after truth could not fail to recognize in it Satan's immediate influence. How could it have happened, then, that six centuries after these strictures the theater so lost its diabolical character that the clergy could call it up within the very Church itself, to a new and temporarily holy life?

And why, if the theater had risen spontaneously from the church service, did the pious Thomas de Cabham in his *Penitential* [2] shake his head over the profession and state of grace of the *histriones*, the actors? At about the same time, in the year 1207, why did Pope Innocent III ban the *theatrales ludi* from the Church which not long before had given form to such stage plays?

These questions may well be answered without difficulty to give confirmation to the accepted conclusion of the origin of modern theater. Until this can be done, however, some doubt about the ecclesiastical origin of dramatic art may be allowed, even though that origin has been canonized in numberless handbooks and textbooks. They do not include, however, the necessary preface or introduction and epilogue or conclusion: the preface should deal with the complete annihilation of theatrical arts by various conciliar bans, in particular, that of the Trullan Synod, held in Constantinople in 692 A.D. [3]

The epilogue should deal with the development of a worldly theater, via comic *intermezzi* and such, from the liturgical drama, which must form a link with our modern theater. Two facts must be considered to-

2. See E. K. Chambers, *The Mediaeval Stage*, Oxford, 1903, II, app. G.

3. J. de Douhet, *Dictionnaire des mystères*, etc. in J. P. Migne, *Nouvelle Encyclopédie théologique*, nouvelle sér. t. 2, XLIII, Paris, 1845.

gether: without a theatrical vacuum in the Middle
Ages, there could have been no growth of an autonomous religious theater; and without the secularization
of religious theater, there could have been no liturgical origin for dramatic art.

But accompanying these inevitable considerations
arise new doubts and new questions. A complete theatrical vacuum from the seventh to the tenth centuries implies the existence of an iron curtain between
Eastern and Western Europe, for we know that the
mime actor lived on and flowered in Byzantium.[4] It
also implies a temporary withering of human instinct,
human tendencies and human capacities whose dis-
appearance is strange, to say the least—the more so as
they later manifest themselves in full power and
strength.

But one thing is sure: only a palpable relic or piece
of contemporary writing dealing with the theater can
be accepted as final proof of its existence. We can
hardly expect the first from the transient art of the
theater; and if we had such a thing in our hands,
what certainty have we that it would be recognized as
a relic of the theater, since we know so extraordi-
narily little about all the cultural forms of that period?
And if one were to build one's conclusions upon
extant manuscripts only, one must—to extend the
argument to other grounds—also conclude that the
only music in Western Europe at that time was sacred
music. The musicologist and anthropologist would
surely question the validity of that conclusion, and we
must allow the theater-historian to ascribe the idea of
a theatrical vacuum to a philologic scholarship lacking
in both human and artistic insight.

4. *Reich*, pp. 48 and 134. See also Allardyce Nicoll, *Masks,
Mimes and Miracles*, New York, 1931, p. 159. For its modern
approach and its illustrative material this book is an important extension and often a correction of Reich's still fundamental
study.

To return to secularization, matters developed surprisingly: as early as 1250, Adam le Bossu wrote his well-constructed play, *Jeu de la feuillée*, so well-constructed, indeed, that it clearly betrays his reliance upon existing tradition. Latin liturgical drama, on the other hand, just as stiff, sober, and primitive as the first examples from the end of the tenth century, continued to exist into the fifteenth and even into the sixteenth centuries, never touched by that process of secularization and never betraying any kinship with the semiworldly theater. There may be answers to these considerations also. Whether they can account for everything, however, becomes increasingly doubtful as the questions multiply—and there are many more than the few we have raised here. Nonetheless, I trust that we have raised enough to justify posing this question: how does this view of the origin of drama come into being and where does it find its corroboration?

We need not look far for the answer, since medieval historiography is so recent in birth. As late as 1809, August Wilhelm von Schlegel[5] could state with authority that there was no drama to be found in all Europe during the Middle Ages. His authority did not last long, however, for soon that nonexistent drama began to appear in published texts with commentary. Romanticism, too, blazed the trail for philology. There is no doubt that these conditions or thoughts gave rise to the recognition of the medieval Church not only as the foster mother of the theater—which for a time and in a certain sense it unquestionably was—but also as the single and total source of an entirely independent dramatic art.

Was it not completely in the spirit of Romanticism to localize the metaphysical origins of art in the Church which also gave form and unity to the whole

5. *Vorlesungen über dramatische Kunst und Literatur*, 1809; Sämmtliche Werke, ed. Ed. Böcking, Leipzig, 1846-47. B. 5.

civilization and culture of the time? Even though Jacob Grimm[6] immediately warned against ascribing so exclusive a derivation to the theater and though Gustav Freytag[7] also pointed to the importance of heathen folk-plays among the recently and summarily converted tribes of Western Europe, Romantic ears refused to listen. When Edélestand du Méril published his excellent *Origines latines du Théâtre moderne* in 1849, the case for the Church as the origin of theater seemed won forever.

This was not merely a result of the Romantic mood of that age. Du Méril's work had been anticipated about ten years before by Charles Magnin's *Origines du Théâtre moderne*,[8] in which he collected the material for the courses he gave at the Faculté des Lettres in Paris. Magnin twice began and twice left unfinished, for some reason or other, this very readable book—and he never reached the Middle Ages. Nevertheless, he stated his theme clearly in the flowery preface and in several articles: just as the great theater of fifth-century Greece had risen out of religious festivals, so a completely new theater was established, "absolument de la même manière," from the festivals of the Christian Church in the tenth and eleventh centuries. Beside the Romantic theory, we have now the theory of analogy; upon these two pillars, speculation on the origin of theater has built itself an edifice of "established fact."

Though Magnin had shown a clear insight into the

6. *Deutsche Mythologie*, Berlin, 1875-78, I, p. 657. *Kleinere Schriften*, Berlin, 1864-90, V, p. 28.
7. *De Initiis Scenicae Poesis apud Germanos*, diss. Berlin (Nietack) 1838.
8. In 1869 he changed the title into: *Les Origines du Théâtre antique et du Théâtre moderne ou Histoire du génie dramatique depuis le Ier jusqu'au XVIe siècle*. Again the book ended at the fall of the West Roman Empire. Articles by Magnin in *Journal de l'Instruction publique*, Paris, 1834-1836 and 1855, and in *Journal des Savants*, Paris, 1846.

portrayal of life as the quintessence of dramatic art, his theory fell into the hands of Marius Sepet, a capable scholar but merely philological in outlook, who recognized signs of drama only in recorded dialogue.[9] To the incalculable damage of theatrical historiography, his viewpoint has been held to this day by most literary scholars. Little thought has been given to the theatrical: the drama is seen only as an autonomous and all-important entity, and research into the nature and circumstances of the theater itself considered almost superfluous. It is apparently difficult to understand that the playwright, like the composer, writes for an instrument with which he is entirely familiar, an instrument which necessarily influences and limits his creativeness.

I am justified, I think, in ascribing another danger to Sepet's publications. The articles he wrote during the last decades of the nineteenth century were collected and published as *Origines catholiques du Théâtre moderne*,[10] a title which suggests that the liturgy from which the theater was recreated is the same liturgy of the Roman Catholic Church that we know today—and which implies that every objection to the theory might be considered an indirect attack upon the Church itself.

In connection with this, let us turn to the excellent, charmingly written study by Léon Gautier, *Histoire de la Poésie liturgique: les Tropes*.[11] Once the theater had been generally recognized to have sprung from the Christian Church, Gautier undertook to discover exactly how and when this birth took place. He found his object in the tropes, particularly the Easter tropes

9. In a later period Oscar Cargill in *Drama and Liturgy*, diss. Columbia University, 1930, fought him with his own philologic weapons; Neil C. Brooks, *Journal of English and Germanic Philology*, XXX, 1931, p. 433, did not approve.
10. Paris, 1901.
11. Paris, 1886.

of the tenth century, with which the names of Tutilo,
Notker, and Radpert are forever associated in men's
minds. How pleasant his humble phrasing is:[12] "Il
convient de voir dans les tropes une des origines du
théâtre moderne. Je n'ose pas dire:—l'Origine—et je
serais cependant tenté de le croire." His small doubt
was soon forgotten by Gautier's followers, however,
and since that time the *Quem quaeritis* trope is stated
in all our textbooks and handbooks to be the source
of modern drama.

But Gautier also made it quite clear that these tropes
were local and private additions to the service, smug-
gled into the liturgy "un peu par contrabande" and
certainly neither recognized nor tolerated by Rome.
We stress this particular result of Gautier's researches,
as it indicates once more the danger in the title Sepet
chose for his collected essays.

Soon another analogy was developed to strengthen
the theory of the ecclesiastical origin of drama. In the
eighteen-seventies the ethnological school arose with
W. Mannhardt's *Der Baumkultus der Germanen*[13]
and E. B. Tylor's *Primitive Culture*. This school
quickly achieved general recognition, particularly with
the publication of Sir James Frazer's *The Golden
Bough*, which continued to ramify from 1891 to
1918.[14] Collection of information concerning the rites
of primitive peoples, research into their origin and
meaning, comparison of these rites with our knowledge of ancient cults and the still evident relics of
Celtic and Germanic religions in Europe opened up
an entirely new field, up to the present only partially
explored. Again and again, ethnology threw new light
upon unsuspected connections and produced surpris-

12. *Op. cit.* p. 138.
13. Berlin, 1875. Further *Wald- und Feldkulte*, 2 Aufl., besorgt
von Dr. W. Heuschkel, Berlin, 1904 and *Mythologische
Forschungen*, Berlin, 1884. 2 vol.
14. First edition 2 vol., third ed. 12 vol.

ing new insights into the spiritual development of mankind. And for love of surprise, indeed, it jumped from time to time to bold conclusions which proved to be valueless.[15]

Perhaps because of this Wilhelm Creizenach speedily freed himself from ethnology with a gracious wave of the hand in his *Geschichte des neueren Drama*, in both the 1893 and 1911 editions. At the same time, however, E. K. Chambers devoted the greater part of his *Mediaeval Stage* to the enumeration of popular customs, more or less theatrical in nature. These afforded him few new conclusions. Lack of new conclusions hardly served as an excuse for H. H. Borcherdt's negation of the new school in his *Europäische Theater im Mittelalter und in der Renaissance*.[16] He deviated from the gladly, though one-sidedly, accepted conclusion from the ethnological school that every religion "est elle-même génératrice de drama et que tout culte prend volontiers et spontanément l'aspect dramatique et théatral," as Gustave Cohen explained.[17] Ethnology proved once more the theatrogenetic character of religion; strengthened by this second analogy, Karl Young could demonstrate in his excellent corpus of liturgical texts, *The Drama in the Medieval Church*,[18] precisely how the drama grew out of the church service.

What has escaped most people, however, is that the word "religion" has completely different meanings

15. We list here only: Hermann Usener, *Arbeiten zur Religions-geschichte*, in *Kleine Schriften*, IV, Leipzig, 1912-13. W. Robertson Smith, *Lectures on the Religion of the Semites*, London, 1889. E. Durkheim, *Les Formes élementaires de la vie réligieuse*, Paris, 1912. L. Lévy-Brühl, *Les Fonctions mentales dans les Sociétés inférieures*, Paris, 1909. G. van der Leeuw, "La Structure de la mentalité primitive," *Revue d'Historie et de Philosophie Religieuse*, VIII, p. 1, Strasbourg-Paris, 1928.
16. Leipzig, 1935.
17. *Le Théâtre en France au Moyen Age*, Paris, 1928, t. I, p. 5.
18. Oxford, 1933, 2 vol.

in the mouth of the ethnologist and in the mouth of the faithful. Can a connection be made between something that springs from the conjuring rites of a totemistic community and the prayers and hymns to the Savior uttered by a Christian congregation? Has the frenzy of the fertility dances in the primitive and ancient world anything in common with the joy of those redeemed from the cycle of life and death and reborn to a Higher Life? Have, then, analogies with primitive cults and Greek religion any value for the thesis that Christianity gave form to a dramatic art?

We could of course reverse the question: if it can be shown how and why drama grew out of the various cults and religions, are the same motivations to drama also present in Christianity, particularly in the liturgy of the medieval Church?

The answer to these questions may prove not without importance to our understanding of dramatic art.

2: The Primitive Phase

THEATER IS play—which defines it neither as real nor as unreal, neither as wise nor as foolish, neither as good nor as bad. Theater serves no practical purpose if judged by the standards of everyday life. It is uncommon, separate. Exclusively for those who similarly separate themselves from life (its participants) does theater become truthful, important, orderly. This holds true, not only for theater, but for all art. It characterizes to a great extent also another human activity—the rite. Here lies our first and most permanent tie between the theater and art on one hand and religion and rite on the other. Everything which "does not belong," which serves no direct purpose in nature, which knows no function in society, which essentially escapes the intellect, belongs to the other side of life, to the "totally different," [1] that has from primitive times been experienced as a supernatural force, usually leading into religion.

As an idea, "play" may escape the meshes of rational definition, but as phenomenon we see it everywhere, always a satisfaction to the human urge for pleasure and recreation. It is apparent that from it in spiritual activity the metaphor, [2] for example, has developed and with that, the entire potentiality for abstract thought, which in turn indicates that not only religion, but also man's entire spiritual life, is unthinkable and impossible without play. Play releases man from the

1. See R. Otto, *Das Heilige. Über das Irrationale in der Idee des Göttlichen und sein Verhältnis zum Rationalen*, 1917, Gotha.
2. See J. Huizinga, *Homo Ludens*, Haarlem, 1938, ch. I.

limits of matter. In stage-play, pleasure lies in imitation, originally of external and tangible existence. By the same metaphoric road,[3] this imitation can reach the entire breadth and depth of human emotion. The theater and the rite meet again in such imitation: in primitive cultures, in fact, they are one and the same.

Huizinga put the question of whether or not the peculiar relationship between play and beauty is the result of the very form and order created by play. It is true, at any rate, that play fences in an area of the imagination in which it creates absolute order, strictly guarded against anything which might disturb the in-lusio, the illusion. In every respect, the order it creates is contrary to the disorder of the imperfect world outside the play area: the contrast is so obvious that it seems willed and purposed. With that observation, play is revealed to serve not only as pleasure but also as protection: it creates order to bring a certain part of the chaotic world under control. Though still far from any practical purpose in everyday life, it acquires with this a certain social or perhaps more psychological function.

Protection manifests itself, for instance, in the play of the children. They play at "getting married," not to imitate what they have seen, but to recreate: in doing this, they organize and arrange things according to their own standard. In some languages, children use a diminutive form for such a situation, as in Dutch bruiloftje, "little wedding." Their play establishes some control over the adult world. That the function of play was originally protective is more especially seen in the play of primitive people, who as adults, of course, reflect in their games the problems of their mature life, the struggle for food and the preservation of life.

To them, the order of nature, the regular succession

3. See Jac. van Ginneken, Gelaat, Gebaar en Klankexpressie, Leiden, 1919, ch. V and VI.

and change of the seasons, is of utmost importance. It makes no difference whether one accepts Frobenius' opinion, that the discovery of nature's succession assailed the emotions of primitive men and "the actual fact of the natural rhythm in growth and decline seized upon their inward understanding and this in its turn led to compulsive and reflex action," [4] or prefers Huizinga's theory that the order of play preceded awareness of natural order which was incorporated into play and portrayed by it. Nearly all primitive people enact the regular changes of nature in their plays,[5] clearly intending to bring under their control elements which they do not dominate and, if necessary, to correct them. In such enactment, the element of play retreats gradually into the background and presentation comes to the fore, to such an extent that we may even speak of vicarious representation in dramatic action. So it coincides with ritual. But there purpose prevails.

Play, however, remains inherent in man, and thus the term *Sacer Ludus*[6] is very appropriate. The joy derived from playing is maintained in ritual and expressed itself as spiritual elevation and exaltation, especially when the *Sacer Ludus* "succeeds" and order is felt to be maintained and protected through the performance of the rite. The degree of emotion, together with the necessary collectivity of the rite and lack of adequate language, forced ritualistic representation into the form of dance.

At this point we must go into greater detail. Primitive man depended upon nothing so much as the order of nature. Although the twentieth century has taught

4. Leo Frobenius, *Schicksalskunde im Sinne des Kulturwerdens*, Leipzig, 1932, p. 142.
5. Frazer, *op. cit. passim*, esp. chapter "The Killing of the Tree-spirit."
6. G. van der Leeuw, *Wegen en Grenzen*, 2 ed., Amsterdam, 1948, p. 107.

many of us the brutality of bare existence, it is still difficult to imagine the perpetual fear in the primitive's life of endless subjection. Now that we can understand a little of such anxiety, we realize that in archaic times every deviation in the natural order brought with it terror and the bitter struggle for life. The primitive somehow had to overpower the force maintaining or disturbing order in nature and to compel it to regulate time and tide so that man might live another year in the jungle. Existence, life, could not be thought of in terms of decades; men managed from season to season, periodically renewing their lease on life.[7] That lease was never bestowed mercifully; it had to be extorted with every ounce of force at the primitive's disposal.

The individual could not achieve success in such an environment. As a matter of fact, he could not even survive alone in the wilderness. If anything were to be accomplished, the community had to do it; and for this reason, primitive men lived a communal existence[8] in which the individual for his own sake as well as for the tribe's had to subordinate his own interests completely. The community fought for the lease on life and won it: over the whole primitive world, the community strove by collective rites to approach and dominate the force which ruled nature.[9]

The circumstances under which the rites were performed make it clear to us with what fear, what intensity, what concentration of power they were performed. The element of adoration is competely lacking.[10] If we use Frobenius' word "Ergriffenheit," we had best translate it as "awe" of the change and

7. Theodor H. Gaster, *Thespis. Ritual, Myth and Drama in the Ancient Near East*, New York, 1950.
8. John Collier, *Indians of the Americas,* New York, 1948, ch. II.
9. W. O. E. Oesterley, *The Sacred Dance. A Study in Comparative Folklore*, Cambridge, 1923, p. 15 seq.
10. Loomis Havemeyer, *The Drama of Savage People*, New Haven, 1916, p. 109.

succession in nature. For the primitives, hope was fervent and endless, but security was unobtainable and the threat of destruction and death never ending.

How could this unknown but ever present force be approached and coerced into order? Language could not yet do it; it was too undeveloped. Even for their own uses, the language of primitives did not extend beyond the primary needs of daily life. Was it not far easier for them to portray the course and suspense of the hunt in a mimic dance after it was over than in the still undeveloped and intractable symbol of the word? When we notice that the American Indians, for example, moved that dance from after the hunt to before it, we know that we have reached the next stage of development, of which the purpose is not to relate what has passed but to dominate what is to come. The Supernatural is still too alien and too different to evolve into an individual or a god, but it was certainly thought of as having human qualities. If it could not understand language, it could at any rate understand reality. The minute imitation of that reality, performed by the community on its own behalf, made the desire of the community perfectly clear.

This is the basis for all sympathetic rites, properly called "charms." In the first place, they explain something and express a wish. More than this, the performers themselves enjoy their imitative dance and conceive of the supernatural forces as also deriving pleasure from watching the performance, which pleasure in turn will bring those forces to quicker compliance and concession. The more ardor glowing in the imitative performance, the greater the results on which the tribesmen may count. There was, as we can see, double reason for performing with heart and soul, and the dances had a frenetic character among all primitive peoples.[11]

11. Oesterley, *op. cit.*, p. 19 seq.

More than this, nothing so transports a person, so enables him to approach and enter into the Supernatural as the rhythm of a dance. "In song and in dance man exhibits himself as a member of a higher community: he has forgotten how to walk and speak, and is on the point of taking a dancing flight into the air." [12] Nietzsche was speaking of Greek archaic man, but there was no essential difference between him and the archaic man of other periods and regions. "Who knows the power of the dance, lives in God," said the mystic Jeladdin Rum, speaking of his dancing Mewlewidervishes.[13] Primitive man had not conceived of the gods, but what could bring him into closer and more intimate contact with that vaguely human Supernatural force than the winging rhythm of the dance? "It grips the soul, and even the soul of the gods.[14]

Frazer noted and set down many of these sympathetic dances.[15] Well-known, among others, are the rain charms, in use among the Indians of the Plains today. In times of continuous drought, the medicine man leads the adult males in a vigorous and lengthy dance around a sacred hill or tree. When the dance has reached its peak, he himself climbs the hill or tree and repeatedly pours water on the ground or on the dancers' heads.[16] It goes without saying that the spirit who enjoyed the dance realizes that he must give rain.

---

12. F. Nietzsche, *The Birth of Tragedy*, transl. Wm. A. Haussmann, Edinburgh-London, 1927, p. 27.
13. Erwin Rohde, *Psyche, Seelenkult und Unsterblichkeitsglaube der Griechen*, 7-9 Aufl., Tübingen, 1921. H. S. Nyberg, *Die Religion des alten Iran*, Leipzig, 1938.
14. G. van der Leeuw, *op. cit.*, p. 87.
15. Frazer, *op. cit.*, ch. "Sympathetic Magic" and "The Magical Control of the Weather."
16. W. Mannhardt, *Wald- und Feldkulte*, I, p. 214 seq. and p. 327 seq. Curt Sachs, *World History of the Dance*, New York, 1937, ch. II.

If he fails to do so, the dance will be repeated over and over again, until the spirit understands either that he must in decency repay the tribe for his pleasure, or (more probably) that the force of the dance must press him to fulfill the dancers' desires.

In archaic societies usually the whole community dances, not just the able-bodied males. The dances are exact—a single misstep and the dance must be repeated from the beginning, to prevent the spirit from becoming confused and to preserve the order of the dance itself. The members of the tribe are therefore trained from infancy, and in the complicated dance forms accompanying a growing culture, a leader is needed who through his special relationship with the Supernatural can give detailed instructions concerning the dance. The priests consequently lead the rites, which remain nonetheless expressive of community desire.

Even more important than these incidental rites was the great drama of what, for centuries, we have casually referred to as "the Year." In the archaic world the return of spring meant no less than the escape from death and the return of hope in life. Naturally enough, the community did everything in its power to facilitate and insure spring's return, when a new lease on life could be taken for another cycle of seasons. In or after the solstice—in what we now call December—an early beginning was made to drive out the enemy, winter, death, after which followed the rites of purification, fasting, and lighting of fires. Februarius was in Rome the time of purification and originally the last month of the year.

Through often repeated communal and mimetic dance-ritual, the tribes did everything they could to attract the new life which they longed to receive. As soon as the spring appeared in nature the entire community hurried to welcome it and strengthen its power by an elaborate representation of its victory over winter and summer. The battle between winter and summer is of primary importance in the development of primitive religion as well as of the theater. Frazer's numerous examples demonstrate how, through annual repetition of these rites, the idea of a definite seasonal change retires to the background and winter-in-general gradually opposes summer-in-general, death opposes life.

And slowly an identification was formed between the community leader in the rites of summer and the new life about to break forth, which must afterwards die down completely before hope might be nursed for a new spring. From this concept arose the performance of the year-king or year-priest, known over the whole world, who overcomes death to bring life. With the approach of winter the year-king himself turns into the daemon of death and must perish in a duel with the champion or king of the next year for life to spring forth anew.

This is not the place to enter into a discussion of the secondary developments of this idea, or of the ways they influence theatrical forms still known to us. It was sometimes possible for a king to substitute for himself a slave or captive alien, a mock-king for a day or more, who had to take over the duties of ruler and enjoy all the king's privileges, after which he was sent to his death, burdened with scorn. The fates of Christopher Sly, Krelis Louwen, and Jeppe-of-the-Hill are less tragic, though all are the descendants of those grossly misused substitutes for the year-king. After the execution, the real king came out of hiding to be honored as the reincarnation of life. In other places, the ruler had to be slain and succeeded by his son; in the blood relationship was expressed the continuity of life. Such succession, of course, led to the institution of sacred and venerated dynasties.

Secondary developments are important in the development of the theater for other reasons, since with them arise the myths which eventually change the character of ritual. The interchange of life and death did not remain the subject of ritual dance, but was replaced by the acts and deeds of a certain priest or king or, finally, god. Though his story was still to some extent a reflection of the old year-drama, he himself received a name and became in some degree an individual; the imagination and memory of many generations could add more deeds, more actions to the basic drama of his existence. This development deeply influenced ritual performance, for in the cult of such a hero, the dancer taking his part was no longer himself, a human being reaching out of himself to the Supernatural, but became the very god, or his enemy, or his son: in short, he attempted to present someone else, to play a part.[17]

It is difficult for modern man to realize the enormous importance of this change—indeed, we can hardly imagine the real significance to archaic man of the mimic dance-rite.[18] We must therefore emphasize once more the fact that for him this was no aimless dance but a carefully-planned portrayal, a reflection of observed natural phenomena. For him, life was too difficult to permit art for art's sake alone: the dance-ritual was a means of entering the Unseen by force, of driving one's way into the Power over the world, to capture for oneself some participation in that Power. If the primitive had not been convinced that he could achieve this result through his dance, the rite would have been no rite, but merely dance. But ritual cannot exist without a practical purpose.

Every believer, no matter how simple or how exalted, is tempted by doubt. It should not surprise us, then, that even in the trance of his communal dance-

17. See Th. H. Gaster, *op. cit.;* also Jane E. Harrison, *Ancient Art and Ritual,* New York-London, 1913.
18. Cecil J. Sharp and A. P. Oppé, *The Dance,* London, 1924, p. 4 seq.

rite, primitive man sometimes had difficulty in accepting the efficacy of those things which he so dearly wished to believe: union with the world-force, his ability to make the Unseen visible to his fellow-believers through the medium of his dance. Therefore he put on a mask: the bigger, the more exalted that mask was, the more the onlookers and other dancers were confirmed in their identification of the wearer with, let us say, the rain-daemon.

Their belief in its turn would work upon him, so that their greater intensity in the performance of the ritual would complete, beyond all doubt, the desired union within himself. The mask was thus a matter of prime importance in the accomplishment of unification with the mighty Power.

Among primitive men the belief was widespread that every living creature manifested itself in dual shape. This held good not only for the visible aspect of nature, but also for the invisible aspect; and in this concept originated, as a sort of safety measure, the frequently used double mask. On the one hand, the mask protected the dual manifestation of the man who wore it; on the other, it captured the daemon he portrayed: an explanation which should make clear why, among some primitive peoples, the mask almost automatically caused the union of its wearer with the daemon.

In the history of the theater the double mask has played but a minor role, at least so far as ancient and western cultures are concerned. The single mask, on the other hand, remained exceptionally important until the end of the classical period and was found in the later period, for example, in the *commedia dell' arte*. It developed from archaic times in the change from nature-rite to myth-cult and finally came to portray an individual: the king, the hero, and at last the god celebrated in the myth. With this, its function changed as well. For the actor, it became an external expedient to characterize the figure he represented; at the same time, it long maintained something of its hieratic character in the eyes of the onlookers and served as a *trait d'union* between cult and stage. For precisely the same reasons, the sacred garments worn in the cult were retained in the Greek theater.

Although the development toward mythical rite implied a far-reaching change, the subject of the portrayal remained more or less the same. Again and again we encounter the struggle between life and death, with destruction on one side and resurrection on the other. When portrayal by representation replaced action *in concreto*, the mimicking rite could gradually adjust itself to the myth's essential miracle. A year-king or year-priest who was slain and lived on in his successor gave way to a hero or demi-god—in the ancient world, for example, Hercules. Finally it was the god himself who died, went to the realm of the dead, to return again for his resurrection. This imagery, indeed, comes closer to the original vegetation-subject than the old rite did, with its protagonist and antagonist. It is understandable that in the development of ritual drama toward the mythical religions, such as those of the Near East, rite and myth merged, and many scholars feel that this is what took place in prehistoric Greece. In any case, with these religions we have definitely passed out of the primitive phase.

In addition to the year-rite and the manifestations of sympathetic magic, the archaic period provided frequent opportunity for the mimic dance to develop out of the complexities of religious consciousness. Hunting and war dances were designed to bring good luck and were thus to some extent charms. The same does not hold true for the initiation rites, performed when youths were inducted into tribal adulthood. The initiators as well as the initiated considered this a turning point in the lives of the young men; more than that, it was for them a departure from an old life and the undertaking of a new one—as many initiation rites clearly indicate, a kind of rebirth.[19]

Introduction into the secrets of life and their meaning belonged, of course, to initiation. Almost always, the mimic-dance took over from a language as yet too little developed to describe all the secrets passed on by the tribe to the young men. The initiation continued to develop itself, too, and in a much later phase the initiation dance was often so lost in conflicting and confusing symbolism that only the priest could explain its ancient meaning. At this point, its original function, that of teaching the inexperienced, had disappeared entirely, and in turn language, now fully developed, was called in to assist; explanation by the initiating priest became the rule.

There is certainly some question as to whether or not these rites, in addition to expressing the urge to mimic, also served as occasions for joy, pleasure, and imitation for its own sake. In any case, they do not compare with the year-play as a propelling force in the development of drama. They are worth considering here, though, because of the influence they exercised and because of the importance some scholars have attached to them.

All these rites, their developments and secondary aspects, may seem remote to us, but Europe is full of relics of similar archaic cults. Its literature may not give much evidence of this, but we must bear in mind that in the history of mankind, literature belongs only to the most recent period. Still, at the beginning of vernacular literature in Europe we have the *Jeu de la feuillée*, by Adam le Bossu, and somewhat later, in the Hulthem Manuscript (conservatively dated about 1375) the *Abel spel vande Winter ende Somer* (Noble play of Winter and Summer), whose close ties—however far their form from archaic rites—with the year-

19. Jane E. Harrison, *Themis*, 2 ed., Cambridge, 1927. George Thomson, *Aeschylus and Athens*, London, 1941.

drama cannot be denied. Again, clear traces of rites are to be found in the English mumming-plays, which belong more to folklore than to formal literature.

In his *Golden Bough*, James Frazer collected a treasury of European folk customs that clearly go back to fertility rites;[20] and the results of later researches make it clear that these same rites were customary among the oldest tribes of Europe,[21] and in turn among the generations following them. What else can we expect, after all, since the struggle for life changes so little because of different climates or continents?

A single example should suffice; in various districts of Europe, particularly in southern Germany, at the approach of spring the men (sometimes only the bachelors) customarily carry winter, or death, out of their village in the shape of a monstrous straw doll. With much noise, they throw the doll into the water, sometimes even burn it, but not before its women's clothing has been removed. This execution is always accompanied by a round-dance. The clothes become in turn the symbol of continuity and are put on a maiden, colorfully adorned. Garlands deck her hair, and she is carried in triumph to the village amidst the cheers and shouts of the villagers. This folk custom, apparently so simple and happy, is directly descended from the bloody rites of which we spoke earlier.

We must observe that such customs were not written down and described before the nineteenth century, which indicates that many traditions continued to exist through the years in different forms and disguises, without leaving the slightest trace in writings and archives. The cultural historian particularly must constantly keep this fact in mind.

20. Frazer, *op. cit.*, v. IV, p. 233 seq., p. 247, p. 249 seq., p. 260, p. 264 seq.; v. IX, p. 404 seq.; v. X, p. 119 seq.
21. O.a. Bertha S. Phillpotts, *The Elder Edda and Ancient Scandinavian Drama*, Cambridge, 1920. Vilhelm Grønbeck, *The Culture of the Teutons*, London, 1931.

It is clear from the foregoing survey that in the rites of archaic religion there was plenty of opportunity for the exercise of the human urge to mimetic play. This germ of theater was particularly developed in the year-play, though it was unable to expand into an independent expression and its ritual characteristics never disappeared. Its performance was an action in itself and had a prescribed purpose: it was not a mental commemoration; it was an act of identification carried out in energetic ecstasy by the entire tribe or community. Through this autonomous act, it aimed at obtaining for that group a part in the Supernatural, at extorting demands from the Power-over-Life. With the appearance of myth, that development began which eventually led to the separation of ritual and theater.

3: The Archaic Phase

FERTILITY RITES, the combat between winter and summer, and initiation rites are found, necessarily with variations, over the whole world. Change is not in the nature of these rites, and their fixed forms vary only under the pressure of centuries or of invasions. Europe still swarms with original folk-customs today, although it was very efficiently cut off from its pagan origin by the penetration of Christianity and the rise of the new civilization accompanying Christianity. We can therefore expect no startling changes in the transition from the primitive to the ancient phase; changes appear only gradually.

We need not be surprised, then, that Kurt Sethe[1] set back the date of the Egyptian king-drama that he discovered and published from its scribal year, 1970 B.C., to approximately 3300 B.C. That drama includes all the rites familiar to us—the duel, the burial of the old king, his resurrection in his successor and the installation of the new king; in addition, the sacramental meal and all the other ceremonies designed to spread the power, the mana, over the earth. The same material exists in other texts published by Sethe and in the drama of Ras Schamra as well.[2]

They all belong to the myth-cycle of Osiris, who was, among other things, god of fertility and life. He

1. K. Sethe, *Dramatische Texte zu Alt-Aegyptischen Mysterienspielen,* Leipzig, 1928.
   Id. Die Alt-Aegyptische Pyamidentexte, 4 vol., Leipzig, 1908-22. See also George Freedley and Joh. A. Reeves, *A History of the Theatre,* New York, 1941, p. 1-8.
2. J. Friedrich, *Ras Schamra,* Leipzig, 1933.

was treacherously murdered by his brother Seth, but his son Horus in turn defeated Seth by force and succeeded him. As widespread were the myths of Isis' mourning for Osiris, the division of his body—a paraphrase of the sacramental meal—and of Isis' sorrowing journey over the earth, a journey which could end only in Anubis' recalling her dead husband to life.[3]

A description of a Near Eastern pantomime-play has been preserved which tells of the suffering of the god Bel,[4] who went to the underworld and was resurrected after three days; from time immemorial this play was put on in Babylon on New Year's Day. Then there is the Asif, autumn-feast of the Hebrews, in which, among much else, the struggle between a god and a dragon is portrayed. From Gaster we learn that all sorts of texts on fertility and seasonal themes must be interpreted as recitatives accompanying pantomimic dances.[5] He himself found several such among the Egyptians, the Hittites, the Babylonians, and the Hebrews.

The Syrians and Babylonians shared the cult of the year-god Tammuz Adon, or Adonis, which appears to have reached Greece by way of Cyprus, where from the seventh century B.C. there were annual celebrations of the death and resurrection of the life-god. Asia Minor, and particularly Phrygia, knew the deeply emotional rites of Attis, who with his god-like mother Cybele was later to create a sensation among the Romans of the third century A.D.

In all rites developed within the mythological framework, there are strong elements of tension and emotion and frequently bloody deeds and merciless acts. The ritual for Attis, for example, proves how

3. See Frazer, *op. cit.*, ch. "Osiris."
4. F. M. Th. Böhl, *Nieuwjaarsfeest en Koningsdag in Babylon en Israël*, Groningen, 1927.
5. Gaster, *op. cit.*, ch. V.

much these rites still meant to priests and performers in the years immediately preceding the advent of Christianity. In emotion, in frenzy, and also in cruelty, they show a close kinship with the worship of Dionysus, a worship which could lead on to further excesses.

Whether his cult sprang from Assyria[6] or from Thrace with Phrygian admixture,[7] is of little importance, really: throughout the Near East it is not with various gods we have to deal, but with various names and with a certain differentiation in rite caused perhaps by tribal consciousness.[8] In any case, the wild worship of Dionysus gained its characteristic form in the Thracian north, from which it spread all over Greece. The Dionysian ecstasy and frenzy, the mania, came to occupy an important place in Greek religion, but that particular ecstasy-in-god would never have been so rapidly and completely accepted if the Greek tribes had not been for some time familiar with such emotion.

The Maenads were certainly new to the courtly Homer, however, and to his rationalistic feudal circle, though for years before his time the maddened women had raged through the mountains of barbarous Thrace, where it was said that the inhabitants greeted death as a liberation. Such an idea was strange to the man who preferred to be hireling to a landless farmer to being lord of the underworld.

The Maenads held their orgies far off on the mountaintops at night, by the flickering light of swaying torches. "The loud and troubled sound of music was heard," said Rohde describing these rites,[9] "the clash

6. C. W. Vollgraff, Ἔριφος ἐς χαλ᾽ ἔπετον, Meded. Kon. Akademie v. Wetensch, afd. lett. 1924, 57, A, Amsterdam.

7. Martin P. Nilsson, *Geschichte der Griechischen Religion*, I (Hand. der Altert. Wiss., V, 2, I), München, 1941.

8. Cf. George Thomson, *op. cit.*, p. 109 seq. and ch. VIII.

9. Erwin Rohde, *Psyche*, quoted from the English translation by W B. Hillis, London, 1925, p. 257.

of bronze cymbals; the dull thunderous roar of kettle-drums; and through them all penetrated the 'maddening unison' of the deep-toned flute, whose soul Phrygian *auletai* had first waked to life. Excited by this wild music, the chorus of worshippers danced with shrill crying and jubilation. We hear nothing about singing: the violence of the dance left no breath for regular songs. These dances were something different from the measured movement of the dance-step in which Homer's Greek advanced and turned about in the *Paian*. It was in frantic, whirling, headlong eddies and dance-circles that these inspired companies danced over the mountain slopes. They were mostly women who whirled around in these circular dances till the point of exhaustion was reached; they were strangely dressed; they wore *bassarai*, long flowing garments, as it seems, stitched together out of fox-skins; over these doe-skins, and they even had horns fixed to their heads. Their hair was allowed to float in the wind; they carried snakes sacred to Sabazios (i.e. Dionysus) in their hands and brandished daggers or else thyrsos-wands, the spear-points of which were concealed in ivy-leaves. In this fashion they raged wildly until every sense was wrought to the highest pitch of excitement, and in the 'sacred frenzy' they fell upon the beast selected as their victim and tore their captured prey limb from limb. Then with their teeth they seized the bleeding flesh and devoured it raw."

It is no surprise to note that it was usually a bull or other animal that represented the god: the eating of the god by his followers, which spread his force over the whole world, is a common detail of many fertility rites. In such a case excitement leading to frenzy is deliberately sought and intended, just as it had been in primitive ritual dance. "Violently induced exaltation of the senses had a religious purpose, in which enlargement and extension of his being was man's only way, it seemed, of entering into union and relationship

with the god and his spiritual attendants."[10] The god
is naturally presumed to be present in many forms,
but sometimes only in the form of the bull; wild
convulsive attempts at union with him lead, then, to
the *omophagia* (eating of the flesh) mentioned before.[11]

But the frenzy is spiritually directed: the soul de-
parts from the body in order to enter into godhead.
The words "ecstasis" and "enthousiasmos" pertain to
the blessed state reached by tearing the man from his
everyday self and flinging him into the state of godhead. When he can do this, then the streams will run
with milk and honey and earthly existence become
eternal bliss, as Plato relates in his *Ion*.

Emergence, awakening from such frenzy brings
no backsliding, no disenchantment, for the memory
remains of a paradise-existence by which the soul is
purged. "When she awakes she can return with un-
encumbered soul to normal everyday life." [12]

It becomes clear that the mania is a direct result of
man's desire to awaken that mania. The breaking away
from ordinary existence, the segregration of the
thiasos, the group of Maenads, raging through their
dim, unrecognizable world, and above all, the liberat-
ing rhythm of the dance—these were the effective,
carefully chosen aids to reaching that state in which
man breaks out of himself and goes over into godhead
to taste the eternity of a blessed earthly life. It is
understandable that when the Dionysus-worship spread
into Greece, its tide suddenly became a flood: for this

10. *Ibidem*, p. 258.
11. Martin P. Nilsson, *A History of Greek Religion*, Oxford,
1949, p. 205: "This sacramental meal is the supreme mystery,
through which the worshippers receive the god and his power
into themselves. Like all primitive cults this one had originally
a practical purpose, which evident indications show to have
been the arousing of the fertility of Nature."
12. U. von Wilamowitz-Moellendorf, *Die Glaube der Hel-
lenen*, Berlin, 1932, II, p. 60 seq.

cult was open to everyone; no priest guarded it and allotted grace. Anyone who wished could participate in it, and anyone might reach ecstasy. Dionysus was the god of the masses.

Still another reason contributed to the popularity of Dionysus-worship. Perhaps without even realizing it themselves, the masses recognized in his worship something of their own fertility-rites; perhaps from those rites the phallos, a symbol in Greece long before Dionysus, passed into the procession of the *thiasos*. Even in Athens the phallos[13] remained inseparable from all the manifestations of the Dionysus cult, including the theater.

Later a strange rumor became current in Greece; the grave of Dionysus was to be found in the temple at Delphi—though no one had ever seen it. This story illustrates the process of extension to which the god was subject—his identification with other gods, already known, in whom the fertility-daemon was still felt to some extent; and so the Dionysus-myths developed. Some foreign influences may have made themselves felt as well—for instance, the worship of the child Dionysus may have been imported from Lydia.[14] In any case, the child Dionysus was annually summoned to life at Delphi and rocked there in a winnow. The use of a winnow as cradle was certainly not unknown, but the combination of an instrument to purify seed with a fertility-god indicates an intrinsic connection with fertility-rite.

Dionysus was not, however, merely a fertility-daemon: everyone knows him as the god of wine. In the Anthesteria-festival[15] Athens honored him as the god of spring and growth; by the end of the archaic period he was associated with the worship of

13. Nilsson, *History*—
14. Nilsson, *Geschichte*—
15. Gilbert Murray's "Introduction" to Gaster's *Thespis;* Nilsson, *Geschichte*, p. 551.

the dead. His origin was too complex to allow him only one shape. But in whatever form he appeared, he stimulated an orgiastic state, while his following was characterized by the phallos-attribute.

The myths at the base of the Orphic mysteries, dedicated to Dionysus, also indicate their origin in fertility-rite and year-drama. Like the figure from whom they took their name, Orpheus, they were of Thracian origin, though a comparison with the Osiris-myth suggests the unimportance of different localities. Dionysus was set upon and torn to pieces by the Titans, as Osiris by Seth. Again, the heart of the murdered Dionysus was saved and eaten by Zeus, who begat him again on Semele. As in many myths of impregnation of the earth by the sun, the mother was disgraced and the child secretly brought up in a distant place. Here, then, is the "liknites" (the man of the winnowing fan) rocked in the winnow-cradle at Delphi and later brought out before the public.

In the Orphic mysteries this may have served as symbol for the separation of body and soul, for the destruction of the flesh and the triumph of the immortal and divine soul;[16] but such exegesis is necessarily of much later date, for the myth itself clearly reflects the year-drama, here reaching out of its primitive phase deep into its ancient phase. Also in its second stage, theater rose out of it.

But before we focus our attention upon this development, let us look at the situation at the end of the classical period, when the Dionysian mania had long been diked into the official channels of a clerical hieromania. The wild god was quartered at Delphi, where Apollo civilized him—but not without catching some of his contagious fire, for the mantic culture which began to blossom at Delphi retained as its core the Dionysian ecstasy.

16. G. van der Leeuw, *op. cit.*, p. 69.

In the migration of the late archaic period, Athens, spared from foreign influx, held off the licentious god for some time and never knew such extreme passions of his cult as the rest of Greece. The Great Dionysia, for example, supposedly imported by Pisistratus, were celebrated during the day, and a veneer of gaiety and light gave an entirely different aspect to the old symbolic apparatus of the nocturnal cult. Such at least is the picture we get from official reports.

But Athens knew and experienced more of the Dionysian mania than these reports indicate, as the success in 405 B.C. of Euripides' *Bacchae* certainly indicates. It is worth attention that it was Euripides, the all-searching, all-questioning tragedian, who provided testimony of thorough acquaintance with the Dionysian mania. Even more telling, perhaps, is the reaction of the Athenian audience, which cheered his posthumous work with tremendous enthusiasm. For those who know Dionysus only as the pretty, friendly young wine-god of a happy spring-festival, Euripides' drama is totally incomprehensible. "Like an irresistible current overwhelming the swimmer, like the mysterious helplessness frustrating the dreamer, the magic power emanating from association with the god took complete possession of the worshipper and drove him whither it willed. Everything in the world was transformed for him; he himself was altered. Every character in the play falls under the spell as soon as he enters the magic circle. Even the modern reader who turns over the pages of Euripides' poem feels something of that strange power to subdue the soul wielded by the Dionysiac mysteries and experiences in his own person a faint reflection of these extraordinary states of mind." [17]

We must realize that Schiller's *Wilhelm Tell*, which rouses every German heart, does not stir a Frenchman

17. Rohde, *op. cit.*, II, p. 47; Engl. transl. p. 286.

for a moment, and the modern reader plods doggedly through T. W. Robertson's *Caste* and Voltaire's *Zaïre*, plays which once kindled flames in the breasts of the generations for which they were written. Mankind in general and the theater public in particular are narrowly bound by the limits of time and place to their immediate environment. With this fact in mind, we return to Euripides' *Bacchae* and realize that the play could have caused such great emotion in its audience in 405 B.C. only if the audience had a close tie with and thorough knowledge of the subject, of the Bacchic essence. Its testimony, even though of a much later date, is sufficient to remove all doubt that in the early times which gave birth to drama in Greece the Dionysian cult was known in Athens as in the rest of the country.

Moreover, not Arion, nor Thespis, nor Archilochos, constantly referred to by the Greeks as the founders of tragedy, was born or raised in Athens. Many places in the Greek provinces, especially in the Peloponnesus and Megara, claimed the honor of first producing tragedy; and from one of these places the art was imported into Athens, where it reached its fullest bloom in antiquity.

We lack precise facts about the origin of tragedy. The oldest source is Aristotle's *Poetics*. Aristotle had without doubt an extensive knowledge of the Greek theater and had seen or read some two hundred and fifty Greek plays.[18] Even in his own time he was famous for his scholarship and undoubtedly had access to all sorts of official archives.[19] Even though by the fourth century B.C. the period decisive for the origin of Greek dramatic art was long since past, his statements must be our final authority.

The origin of tragedy, unlike the origin of comedy,

18. Only thirty-three are known to us.
19. A. W. Pickard-Cambridge, *Dithyramb, Tragedy and Comedy*, Oxford, 1927, p. 122.

appears to have been well known to him, but what he says of it is, for us late-comers, so little and so vague that as many interpretations have arisen as there have been commentators on the *Poetics*. Nothing can be gained by throwing ourselves into this melée. Nonetheless, we can observe it with profit, for the whole chaos of misunderstanding results from a quest for truth and knowledge about the Greek theater. If King Juba II's *Theatrike Historia* should ever be found, which described in the first century A.D. in seventeen volumes the development of dramatic art, how rapidly the learned storm would die down and Aristotle's meanings be clarified.

The Greek philosopher says that tragedy "certainly began with improvisations—just like comedy; the former rose out of the leaders of the dithyramb and the latter from phallic songs which still exist as institutions in many of our cities." [20] In classical Athens the dithyramb was a song always in honor of but not always about Dionysus, a song full of the springtime joy; such for instance is Pindar's first dithyramb. It was called "the fair song of Dionysus"; and Archilochos of Paros told how in 675 B.C., when he was archon, he sang the dithyramb when drunk. Drunkenness was admirably suited to the accompaniment of the Phrygian flute, described by Aristotle as "orgiastika kai pathetika": wild and passionate. It is quite likely that the song and its accompaniment belonged to the wild rites in Thrace even before Dionysus arrived in Greece.

How remote this is from the well-trained choruses of carefully chosen boys who sang and danced around the flutists and the altar in the orchestra of a fifth-century Athenian theater! The prize in their contest was a bull or a goat, such as the one Thespis is supposed to have won about 534 B.C. [21] The name of the

20. *De Poetica*, 1449.
21. Pickard-Cambridge, *op. cit.*, p. 165.

animal (*tragos*) could have become connected with the new form which Thespis gave to the dithyramb. In this manner, perhaps, the dithyramb became "tragedy."

Or does "tragedy" mean the song of the *tragoi*, the followers of Dionysus, who was slaughtered in his incarnation as a goat by the members of his *thiasos* and eaten in a sacramental meal, so that through this *omophagia* they were united with him and could also call themselves goats? [22] Euripides' *Bacchai* deals with the ritual form of the same union; man's spiritual surrender to the god makes him a daemon, a sacred animal in the god's divine herd. The second derivation has much more significance than the simple gift of a goat as prize; but names originate in singular ways.

According to tradition, Thespis pruned the dance of the *choreutai*, the satyrs or sileni which made up the chorus. They were half-animal, half-daemon and were dressed, like Maenads, in the motley furs of many animals. Goatskins, horsetails, and fox-ears made up their costume, which serves to support Aristotle's suggestion that tragedy was originally satyric.

Thespis did still more: he gave the exarchon, or leader of the chorus (afterwards called *coryphaeus*) the part of *hypokrites*, a word frequently interpreted as responder but better translated as "explainer." Through the various recitations which Thespis assigned him, the exarchon came to represent a certain character.

It is difficult to penetrate the complete darkness of the period before Thespis. According to Aristotle, the language of tragedy in its satyrical phase had been ridiculous in character and was written in trochaic meter to go with the dancing which prevailed until Thespis stepped in. "Satyrical" here means "performed by satyrs." These were nothing more than vegetation-

22. Margarete Bieber, *The History of the Greek and Roman Theater*. Princeton, 1939, p. 22; see also Vollgraff, *op. cit.*

and fertility-daemons dressed in animal skins. For some of these rites form a bridge to the ritual combat of winter and summer as it was performed at Eleutherae. Dionysus, now called Melainaigis,[23] "he in the black skin," assisted at the rite: after the death of winter he participated in the victory. Eleutherae is almost certainly the place from which Dionysus was introduced into Athens. Some idea of the oldest forms of tragedy can be obtained from fifth- and sixth-century vases,[24] many of which picture Dionysus in ecstasy surrounded by wildly dancing satyrs and Maenads.

We have other bridges as well: one of them leads to the primitive initiation rites, where, as we have seen, much representation was often necessary. With much sagacity, Thomson traced the Dionysian *thiasos* back to initiation into tribal secrets and to the group solidarity arising from it. The rites, as we know, formed a mystery comprehensible only to the initiated; when that ritual became drama in its mythological stage, the leader had to give an explanation to the uninitiated audience. For example, when a group danced the wanderings of Eleuther's daughters, driven by Dionysus into madness for scorning him as Melainaigis, their fellow-performers knew precisely what they were doing and whom they portrayed, but the audience had to be told. The exarchon therefore became *hypokrites* and fulfilled the same function as the *exegetes* in the Eleusinian mysteries: he presented himself as Dionysus and drove the women into frenzy. Indeed, as Aristotle had said, tragedy was to be found in the leaders of the dithyramb.

Ethnologists discovered in the regions surrounding Greece still another bridge between tragedy and the tribal year-drama. The Dionysian rites themselves provided ample material for taking this path—as Jane

23. Pickard-Cambridge, *op. cit.*, p. 161.
24. M. Bieber, *op. cit., passim*, o.a. p. 8.

Harrison said,[25] the difficulty lies in the fact that the Greeks transformed all their old rituals into the new dramatic art with such ingenuity that the origin can only be guessed at. This path of guesswork, too, leads to a purely personal interpretation which cannot satisfy every researcher into the question.

But this does not alter the importance of such a theory as Gilbert Murray's.[26] Murray feels that the material of Greek tragedy arises from mythology but that its form goes directly back to the rites for the new year-daemon, who became in many cases a tribal god because of the tribe's regular need for him. Murray called him the *Eniautos Daimoon:* year-spirit.

It now appears that at Delphi so-called *dromena* (things done) were executed—in other words, rites —corresponding to the rites for the year and tribal god. Of that ritual year-drama, exactly the same in nature as the Egyptian Osiris-drama, the struggle, or *agon*, was a relic; so was the suffering and downfall connected with it, which formed the *pathos*, the tale of the messenger, the mourning or *threnos*, the recognition of new life or *anagnorisis;* finally appeared, as an incarnation of renewed life in a young daemon or god, the *epiphany*. Not all these elements, of course, were simultaneously present in the tragedies of the fifth century, but in Murray's opinion there are enough traces to support this conjecture for the development of tragedy.

As soon as the participants in the rites no longer believed in the practical purpose of those rites, the greater part of the community which had originally danced the rites lost the enthusiasm that had once inspired them to take part: they became spectators, and the *dromenon* performed for them became drama.

25. Jane E. Harrison, *Ancient Art and Ritual*, p. 14.
26. Gilbert Murray's "Excursus in the ritual forms preserved in Greek drama" in Jane E. Harrison's *Themis;* see also his "Introduction" to Gaster's *Thespis*.

It is quite understandable that after a loss of faith in the rituals, annual repetition of the winter-summer combat retains little of its original urgency and interest. According to Murray's theory, Dionysian ritual brought new content into ritual in its hour of decay, and through Dionysus contact was established with the other gods as well. It then became possible to draw upon the deep well of the whole mythology, which made the growth and flowering of fifth-century drama feasible—and Aeschylus is said to have called his plays "fragments of Homer's banquet."

Still more bridges were built between tragedy and ancient ritual,[27] but no one will be surprised to learn that not one provided a direct crossing. Comedy was more difficult to trace: even Aristotle admitted that he knew little of its early phases. Comedy as a dramatic form was not taken so seriously as tragedy, and he devoted less attention to it. All he could say was that improvisation and phallic song are the two elements from which it springs, that the Dorians of Megara claim the first comedy, and that its name derives from their villages, the *komai*.

Before Attic comedy came into existence, Dorian burlesques were known all over Greece, and Megara was clearly the center of their growth. The characters in those plays were farce-types, among which the Hercules-figure was most important. There are, furthermore, indications that the dance was the origin of Doric mime. All these fairly loose data,[28] together with the remnants in the Old Comedy of animal choruses, obscene expressions, and aggression in the parabasis, the oldest element of the play, clearly sug-

27. See o.a. von Wilamowitz, *op. cit.*, p. 92 seq.
28. Comp. Heinz Schnabel's remarkable essay *Kordax: Archae-ologische Studien zur Geschichte eines antiken Tanzes und zum Ursprung der Griechischen Komödie*, München, 1910.
    See also: H. Reich, C. Magnin, A. W. Pickard-Cambridge, M. Bieber, *op. cit.* and esp. A. Nicoll, *op. cit.*, ch. I, 2 and p. 83.

gest an origin which in tumult and ferocity is not far from the "orgiastika kai pathetika" of dithyrambic flute and Dionysian cult. For most scholars, the connection seems completely acceptable.

In early times the parabasis may have been a procession of masked *komastes* who drunkenly insulted their fellow-citizens, carried the phallos and sang songs in honor of a fertility god; that procession was to become part of the rural Dionysia held in the month of Poseidon, where Dionysus himself was identified with the fertility god and his wild revelers dressed up as sileni and pressed around the ship-carriage that had carried him from overseas.[29]

Another explanation is possible as well: some believe that comedy originated directly in the ritual combat of Winter and his following against the New Life and his henchmen, which also provides an *agon, pathos*, death, and resurrection for the *Eniautos Daimoon*.[30] This conjecture, at any rate, provides a common origin for tragedy and comedy, as did no less a critic than Aristotle, who spoke vaguely on the subject and suggested "improvisation" as a starting point for both. Beside these forms—or between them—the satyr-play helped strengthen the tie with the older traditions.

Here again no certain truth emerges from the clash of opinions, and the most we can hope to attain is a considered personal judgment. Our curiosity is kept alive by the valuable clues which remain in the drama. We know the conditions under which the development began and the boundaries of that development, but it is still a riddle as to exactly how Greek drama originated from its primitive phase.

The riddle aspect cannot be overemphasized, since

29. Von Wilamowitz, *op. cit.* In Western Europe, however, the ship-carriage presented a symbol of fertility.
30. Francis M. Cornford, *The Origin of Attic Comedy*, London, 1914.

it was by analogy with the ancient theater that Magnin, Sepet, Cohen and other medievalists developed
their theories of the origin of modern drama and
theater. A riddle gives little support to theories, however; and when Thomson and several other classicists
reverse the analogy and use medieval developments
to support their theories of classical drama, then such
assistance can hardly be called effective.

So far as I know, there is no doubt that ancient
drama grew out of religion, but so long as we do not
know *how* that phenomenon took place, the fact itself
is of no value in the interpretation of a similar art
developing in a later period and under different circumstances.

What has value, on the other hand, is the comparison of cults and religions the theatrogenetic character
of which has been recognized. We arrive at this
question: what is the relation of the rites of primitive
religions to those of archaic Hellas and the later worship of Dionysus?

A comparison yields striking similarities: in the first
place, both cases are mass movements, community expressions in which theatrical elements are manifest.
Either a whole tribe worked itself up into a frenzy,
or a group, which with or without initiation ceremonies stood open for everyone to join. A second
similarity is the wild and frenzied dance born of this
ecstasy, a dance in each case with an extremely pronounced portraying character, on the one hand reflect-
ing emotional tension, on the other indicating by
mimesis the forces so stirring to the emotions. It appears from this that not only do the forms run parallel,
but that the aim is identical: in both cases ecstasy aims
at communion, union with the Invisible, the metaphysical Power, the Deity.

This brings us directly to the fourth similarity,
which lies in the very nature of that ecstasy—that it
is not bestowed upon man by any external mercy or

grace. On the contrary, he must concentrate all his force and power to obtain the rapture which will overmaster the deity and secure for him the communion for which he hungers. Both cases involve man's act, man's deed, through which he acquires—or rather takes—godhead. His rites therefore do not implore, do not accept submissively, do not commemorate in adoration.

The fifth similarity between the primitives and the ancients is that this very ecstasy aroused by the rites leads into portrayal, the core and primary characteristic of dramatic art. Through ecstasy, as the word itself indicates, the cultist can step outside of himself and start on the road to the presentation of other characters.

Presentation can never be ascribed solely to the rapture which lifts man out of himself. Beside the difference in rite and ritual, there is for every man the play-instinct, the instinct of *homo ludens* seeking his pleasure in imitation of what exists. The connection between play and religion is, of course, essential in the history of man's spiritual development.

And this brings us to the sixth point of similarity: in archaic rites and in the Dionysian cult it is not the spirit, not the soul which seeks to approach the Invisible and to receive communion with the Supernatural through prayer, contemplation and renunciation of the world. It is the lust for life, fighting for continuation of its often perilous yet ever-desired existence that strives for an eternal earth overflowing with milk and honey, a satisfaction to all the senses.

4: The Trope

FOR SOME PEOPLE the law formulated by Gustave Cohen holds true: that every religion spontaneously produces drama, every religious service shows by its own nature dramatic and theatrical aspects. No matter how sharply and consistently Christian authority condemned contemporary expressions of theatrical art, even the medieval Church obeyed Cohen's law. Spontaneously, of its own volition, it created entirely new drama: just as in heathen religions, drama rose out of the essential nature of the Church, independent of outside influence. Whence could such influence have come, since the Concilium Trullanum had definitely pronounced the death sentence on the theater, which had therefore vanished about the year 700 A.D.?

We know, too, that the spontaneity Cohen speaks of was held back for several centuries in the case of Christianity, unexpectedly to loose its full force at the end of the tenth century. There is, of course, the fourth-century record of a Galician noblewoman describing her pilgrimage to the Holy Land, the *Aetheriae Peregrinatio*,[1] in which Aetheria mentions ritual dialogues performed by the Christian congregations in Palestine at Christmas and at Easter. This is, however, exceptional: not only in time but also in place it is so far removed from the Church in Western Europe, on the point of creating a new theatrical art, that her account can hardly be of great importance. Moreover, dialogue and drama are far from identical.

It is important, though, to stress geographical loca-

1. *Silviae vel potius Aetheriae Peregrinatio ad loca sancta*, ed. W. Heraeus, Heidelberg, 1908.

tion to make one realize that the Byzantine Church, in contrast to the Roman, has never been described as theatrogenetic. Such description would have been difficult to substantiate, for spontaneity could hardly be proved there. From the beginning, Byzantium had been neighbor to the Greek theater, and in spite of the edict of the Trullan Synod, mimes maintained an active existence in Byzantine society.[2] Much of the ancient theater was preserved in the mime-play; the ninth-century drama, *Christos Paschoon*, clearly depends upon existing forms.[3]

In contrast to the obscurity in the development of the Greek theater, the forces which collectively caused the rise of drama in the medieval Church of Western Europe seem thoroughly known. After thirty years of research and study, Léon Gautier made known his definitive conclusions in his book on the tropes. Almost fifty years later, the American scholar Karl Young published an indispensable collection of extant liturgical texts, arranged according to the opinions he had built up in many articles. His extensive study covers the entire field, and nothing seems to have escaped his searching eye—except the need on the part of readers and critics for a clear annotation of dates.

As we have said, both writers concluded that the germ of the new drama, and with it the new theater, lies in the tropes, particularly in the tropes sung until daybreak during the night before Easter. The first line of that trope was almost invariably the same:

Quem quaeritis in sepulchro, o Christicolae?

In answer to the angel's question followed:

Jesum Nazarenum crucifixum, o coelicolae.

2. See H. Reich, *op. cit.*, p. 202 and A. Nicoll, *op. cit.*, p. 200 seq.
3. Ed. J. G. Brambs, Leipzig, 1885.

Immediately after this interchange, the announcement of Christ's resurrection led to the jubilation of the *Te Deum*.

The origin of this hymn could not have been much later than the tenth century—a late date for the origin of theater if one assumes that every religion is responsible for its birth. Christianity, after all, had been officially established for some centuries in Western Europe. It is indeed a late date when one considers the amount of dialogue in the Gregorian liturgy and the number of voices it required—the very signs serving many scholars as clear manifestations of drama.[4] How are they reconcilable with so late a birth?

Confusion about the appearance of theatrical material is endless and can be laid to the fact that for many scholars drama is only a form—indeed, a typographical form—by which an author conveniently illustrates a conversation. To call dialogue the only indication of drama is like calling rhythm the only indication of music. One of Young's great merits is that he freed himself from such misconceptions and, before doing further research in this material, he first formed clear ideas on the nature and substance of theater.

Quite properly, he rejected dialogue and changes of voice as essential manifestations of drama and recognized only impersonation. With this as his yardstick, he found that the germ of drama was present neither in the Mass nor in any other part of the official liturgy.

After our preceding exposition, it should be clear that the celebrating priest in the Church did not *portray* but *represented*: his medium was not creative acting but commemorative symbolism. The effectiveness of the symbolism depended upon acceptance of

4. See f.i. "Drames liturgiques et jeux scolaires" in M. Sepet's *Origines*.

the doctrine it accompanied, and this clearly indicates its difference from creative acting. Any attempt towards identification with the Unseen, such as we observed in primitive rites, is quite out of the question in the Christian Church.[5]

Symbolism too is an expression of *homo ludens*, a metaphorical game without which abstraction of thought and belief would escape mankind. Though this common factor separates both the priest and the actor from ordinary existence, it no more equates them than the word "play" can equate the practice of a musician and the practice of a tennis player. Even though likeness is an integral element of both symbolism and the theater, it does not bring them closer together: symbolism uses the image of reality to convey an idea and, like all rites, has a purpose. The actor observes only so that he may create afterwards, quite without ulterior or practical purpose. If he loses sight of reality, his art cannot exist. Symbol on the other hand, is constantly in the process of becoming pure idea, of completely shedding its function as image. It lies deep in its nature that its ties with reality must constantly be renewed.

It does not surprise us at all to observe this process taking place in medieval liturgy. In the ninth century, for instance, Amalarius of Metz warned in the preface

5. That the Church never accepted any identification of the officiating priest with Christ, not even in the Consecration, is clearly shown by Dr. Franz Ser. Renz in *Die Geschichte des Messopfer Begriffes*, I, p. 530 (Freising, 1901); see also l'Abbé Louis Duchesne, *Origines du Culte chrétien*, 5th ed., p. 168 (Paris, 1925; Eng. transl. *Christian Worship*). While Christ uses the priest here as His direct instrument in the same way as a writer uses his pen, the priest is in the other parts of the Mass the spokesman for the worshipping congregation and the leader of the commemorative symbolic action. It is the Church's dogma that this symbolism becomes reality when Christ Himself through the miracle of the transubstantiation repeats His eucharistic sacrifice.

to his *De Ecclesiasticis Officiis* that the sacraments must have a certain resemblance to those things which they shadowed forth. Two centuries later Honorius of Autun repeated the warning in his *Gemma Animae*[6] and, in his own reference to the actor, demonstrated particularly the fundamental difference between symbolic representation and mimic portrayal.

He said that the celebrant in the Church, just like the actor in the theater, must present through his gestures Christ's struggle. Honorius' precise directions follow: when the priest says "Orate," he portrays Christ in the Garden of Gethsemane charging the apostles to pray; his moments of silence during the service reflect Christ the quiet lamb being led to slaughter; the stretching out of his arms, Christ's hanging on the cross; his singing of the *Praefatio*, Christ's cry from the cross; the silent prayer of the orisons in the canon of the Mass, the Holy Saturday; and so on.

To us it is plain that Honorius, like many modern interpreters of the divine service, has confused likeness with substance, for the essence of this symbolism has nothing to do with mimic portrayal. Mimic portrayal can never be saved by vague likeness; if it wishes to exist or to continue to exist, it must be a precise portrayal.[7]

It is interesting, moreover, that there remains a faction in the Church that continues to stress this very idea of likeness. This proves that there were opposite groups for whom likeness was unnecessary here: a symbol was sufficient for them as an idea. We see all about us the same development in language when a

6. *De Ecclesiastics Officiis:* J. P. Migne, *Patr. Lat.*, LV and *Gemma Animae*, *P.L.* CLXXII. See also Young, *op. cit.*, I, p. 81 and p. 83.
7. This is true also for theater dominated by emblematic conventions.

metaphor ceases to awaken an image and merely expresses a meaning.[8]

On the basis of such considerations, Young refused to call the Mass "dramatic" in a purely theatrical sense, and his standard is an accurate one. Even the performances in the Church known as *Depositio Crucis*, when on Good Friday the cross and the host are laid near the altar, and the *Elevatio Crucis*, which follows the first, Young calls "striking examples of symbolism. As liturgical exercises, they are uncommonly tender or vivid or splendid, but they lack the essential of true drama." [9] But that essential he finds, like Gautier, in the Easter-trope. Before the performances of *Elevatio* and *Depositio Crucis*, the *Adoratio Crucis* took place on Good Friday. The ceremony comes from Jerusalem, where Aetheria had witnessed it in the fourth century, and was accepted in Rome in the eighth century, where of all the exercises we have noted, it alone belonged to the official Roman liturgy. In spite of this, it is in the *other* exercises that the origin of theater has been identified.

Young's and Gautier's view may find its confirmation in the account of dramatic activities St. Ethelwold of Winchester gave us about the year 970[10] in his *Regularis Concordiae*. These activities took place at Easter in an English Benedictine monastery and in his opinion derived from Benedictine custom in Hainaut and Flanders.

St. Ethelwold's description is well known: "how on the day on which we celebrate the entombment of our Saviour, to the strengthening of the belief of the igno-

8. Comp. Max Herrmann, *Forschungen zur Deutschen Theatergeschichte des Mittelalters und der Renaissance*, Berlin, 1914, p. 201 seq.

9. K. Young, *op. cit.*, p. 148.

10. O. Cargill, *op cit.*, p. 28 raises doubts on this early date. The most important parts of this passage from *Regularis Concordia* in Chambers, *The Med. Stage*, II, app. 0.

rant masses and the converts," on a certain section of the altar a tomb was made in imitation of the sepulchre, in which two deacons had to lay a cross wrapped in cloth "as though they buried the body of our Lord." Ethelwold, however, devoted less of his attention to this act than to the liturgy which accompanies it, and passes quickly over the elevation.

He went on to describe how on Easter morning, at the third Lectio, a monk with a palm branch in his hand had to sit by the tomb. During the third Responsorium which followed, three other monks approached, behaving as if they were looking for something in that tomb. "All this is done to imitate the angel, who sat by the grave and the woman who came with the aromatic unguents to anoint the body of Jesus." He went on: "When he who is seated by the tomb sees how these three approach him in confusion as seeking for something, he must start singing softly and sweetly: *Quem quaeritis?* When he has sung this to the end, these three must answer him as one: *Jhesum Nasarenum.*" The angel must invite the others to look into the tomb. They set down their thuribles, took up the shroud, stretched it to show that there was no longer anything in it, sang the antiphon *Surrexit dominus de sepulchro*, and put the sheet on the altar. "At the conclusion of the antiphon the prior, sharing in the jubilation for the triumph of our King who conquered death and rose again, must start the hymn *Te Deum laudamus:* and after this beginning let all the bells be rung simultaneously." It was undoubtedly a moving and impressive moment.

St. Ethelwold cited only the first words of question and answer—no more was needed, for every Benedictine knew by heart what was to follow; if not, he could look it up in a troparium. In such a collection of tropes he could find many different types, not only those beginning

Quem quaeritis in sepulchro, o Christicolae?

but also those beginning

> *Quem quaeritis in praesipe, pastores, dicite?*

or

> *Quem creditis super astra ascendisse?*

It was these "versiculi ante, inter vel post alios eccle-siasticos cantus oppositi," as Ekkehard described them in his *Casus Sancti Galli*, which, particularly on holi-days, added luster to the church service. Ekkehard's word "versiculus" can be misleading, for these addi-tions and interpolations in the liturgical text were above all musical in nature; poetically they are, with few exceptions, of little importance.[11]

The legend[12] of the origin of tropes which Ekkehard gave in his history of St. Gall is enlightening of this subject. In the course of the eighth and ninth cen-turies such complicated vocalizations had gathered about the final A of the Alleluia in the Mass that even pupils of the monastery's famous music school could not master its difficulties. Notker Balbulus, who as leader of the learned Benedictine school had helped to create its fame, concentrated day and night upon a method to teach his students these variations: "I have begun to consider by what method I might record these melodies."

Help came to him from outside the monastery: about 860, an antiphonarium[13] was brought from the abbey of Jumièges, near Rouen, which had been

11. See Gautier, *op. cit.*, p. 97.
12. See Julius Schwietering, *Deutsche Dichtung des Mittelalters* (Handb. d. Liter. wisschensch. 23), Potsdam, p. 17 seq. Comp. Robert Stumpfl, *Kulturspiele der Germanen als Ursprung des mittelalterlichen Dramas*, Berlin, 1936, p. 66 seq.
13. An antiphonarium is a liturgical book, official and no longer interpolated, in which all parts of the Mass sung by the choir are written, together with their musical notations. It is now often called a *Graduale* or Gradual. In the case of Notker's book, we should properly speak of a *Troparium*; see Gautier, *op. cit.*, p. 70.

destroyed by the Normans. Notker discovered that
in this book the monks had written words under the
vocalizations, which had apparently helped in the
memorization of the melodies. With his fellow-friars,
Tutilo, Radpert, and Hartmann, Notker began to
write the so-called *prosae* under the Alleluia sequences,
which Tutilo in particular managed to insert into
places in the Gregorian liturgy. In this way he interpolated into the Introit of the Mass a sort of pro-
logue; he found expansions for its various sections and
set these interpolations to *cantilenae* or tropes, which
were either already in existence or invented by him
and his brothers.

Not all the tropes we find here and there in Western
Europe at this time were in dialogue form, like the
Quem quaeritis trope. Many were merely expressions
of pure joy, lyric, and designed to support the music:

> *Dominum veneremur, eia et eia, laudes persolvamus,*
> *canentes: Eia!*

Moreover, dialogue-tropes did not introduce a new
form into the liturgy, which had long contained
question and answer. Among other things, the singing
of the psallentes was in question and answer: two half-
choirs sang the *antiphona* against each other. We can
presume that the tropes in dialogue were performed
in the same way. Of these we must first consider the
trope, probably written by Tutilo, for the Introit of
the third Christmas Mass. It reads as follows:[14]

> *Hodie cantandus est nobis puer, quem gignebat inef-*
> *fabiliter ante tempora Pater, et eundem sub tempore*
> *generavit inclyta mater.*

INTERROGATIO: *Quis est iste puer quem tam magnis pre-*
> *coniis dignis vociferatis? Dicite nobis, ut collauda-*
> *tores esse possimus.*

14. Gautier, *op. cit.*, p. 63.

RESPONSIO: *Hic enim est quem presagus et electus sym-
mista Dei ad terras venturum previdens longe ante
prenotavit, sicque predixit: Puer natus est.*[15]

For those who, like all dutiful clerics, wanted to
"strengthen the belief of the ignorant and converts," [16]
such vivid extension of the church service was undoubtedly a splendid occasion to add more visual education. That the clergy attached considerable weight
to this sort of thing, particularly in an illiterate community, is well known and demonstrated to this day
in the stained-glass windows and other decorations
which every visitor sees in a Gothic cathedral.

We do not know whether the manger had been
introduced into the church by Tutilo's time, though
it could not have taken place much later, for we soon
find the trope:

Quem quaeritis in praesipe, pastores, dicite?

RESPONDENT: *Salvatorem Christum Dominum, infantem
pannis involutum, secundum sermonem angelicum.*

RESPONDENT: *Adest hic parvulus cum Maria matre sua,
de qua dudum vaticinando Isaias dixerat propheta:
Ecce virgo concipiet at pariet filium; et nunc euntes
dicite quia natus est.*

RESPONDENT: *Alleluia, alleluia! Iam vere scimus Christum
natum in terris, de quo canite omnes cum propheta,
dicentes: Puer natus est—*[17]

15. Today we are to sing of the Child whom the Father begat
ineffably before the time was and whom his glorious Mother
bore in time.

INT.: Who is this Child whom you worthily celebrate with
such great praise? Tell us that we too may praise him.

RES.: This is He of whom the far-seeing chosen priest of the
Lord foretold long ago that He would come down upon the
earth and thus he prophesied: a Child is born.

16. Strengthening of the belief of the faithful and alluring the
unbeliever is for Herrad of Landberg in her *Hortus Deliciarum*
the purpose of the Christmas plays.

17. Gautier, *op. cit.,* p. 218.

Whom do you seek in the manger, shepherds, tell us?

(Top left) Dance mask of the forest spirit, Wakash Indians on Vancouver Islands, (above) Dance ornament with double mask, New Hebrides, (left) Double mask from Cameroons, the god of Heaven

*Dance mask of
the Bayakka
in Belgian Congo*

*Double mask,
French Equatorial Africa;
used at coronation
and funeral ceremonies*

(Top) New Mexican deer dancers, Nambi Feast,
(bottom) The horn dance at Abbots Bromley;
from a photograph taken in 1893

(Top) Hunting dance with animal impersonation, Bushman painting near Orange Spring in South Africa, (bottom) Paleolithic deer dancer; cavern of the Trois Frères, Ariège

*(Top) The Dionysian ecstasy; cup of Brygos, Paris,
(bottom) Dionysian Thiasos; amphora, Munich*

(Top) Chorus of birds, from Attic vase, the British Museum, (bottom) The three Mary's and the angel at the Tomb; ivory tablet 12th century, Cologne

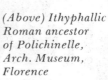

(Top) Medieval mimes in the Byzantine Empire; from a fresco in St. Sophia, Kiev, (bottom) A Roman lamp with mime ancestor of Harlequin; from Pietro Sancti Bartoli

(Above) Ithyphallic Roman ancestor of Polichinelle, Arch. Museum, Florence

(*Top*) *Mimes staging the birth of Helen; vase, Bari,*
(*bottom*) *Mimes burlesque, Leningrad*

(Above) Mimes burlesque: Hermes gives Zeus a light at a nightly visit to Alcmena; vase in the Vatican

(Above) Comic
Roman actor;
marble statuette
from Tralles,
Asia Minor, Museum
at Istanbul;
Photo Giraudon,
(right) Mimes' mask,
larva daemonum;
terra cotta, Bonn

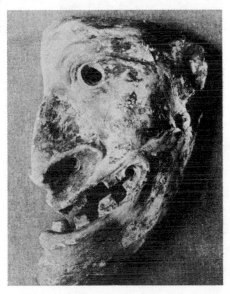

*(Top left) Stupidus; terra cotta, British Museum,
(top right)
Mimes' wisecracking fool
(Bucco?); terra cotta,
British Museum,
(left) Mimes' mask:
he who gets slapped;
terra cotta, Tarentum*

Calliopius surrounded by joculatores and audience;
Terence manuscript, Bibliothèque de l'Arsenal

(Left) King David and
dancing joculatores;
Psalterium Aureum,
St. Gall,
(below) The devils of
mystery plays were
identified with
the demons of the
heathen tradition;
miniature in
Jacob Ruf's play
Von des Herren
Heingarten, 1539

Troparium of St. Martial de Limoges: ball juggling to musical accompaniment by figures in histrionic dress; Bibliothèque Nationale, Paris

Acting figure in histrionic dress; Troparium of
St. Martial de Limoges; Bibliothèque Nationale, Paris

Dancing figure in nonclerical dress and Alleluia sequence;
Troparium of St. Martial de Limoges; Bibliothèque
Nationale, Paris

(Top) Customary play of Winter and Summer, the crowned
wildman and Valentine with ring; woodcut
after Pieter Breughel, about 1560,
(bottom) A demon of the Greek theater;
vase, Kaiser Friedrich Museum, Berlin

This single example may serve to show how a trope developed in the service of a particular commemorative day.

Why did the trope become so fashionable—for so we may call it—in the ninth century? Early in the Christian Church, a desire for renewal and change in the divine service had made itself felt, long before the sixth century, when liturgy received its stable forms.[18] In the fourth century, Arius of Alexandria attempted to enliven the service in a way which led Athanasius to accuse him of apprenticeship to the ungodly mimes. "The meter of various old church hyms," said van der Leeuw, "was borrowed from the mimes' stanza from the time of Gregory Nazianzen, the poet of the famous Evensong."

Even after Athanasius the standard accusation hurled by the councils at the renovators was that they were trying to smuggle scandalous theater-songs into the Church. Nonetheless, conciliar fulmination could not prevent regular intrusion of lay-songs into the divine service. Some clerics had no objection to this introduction and adopted the songs liberally into their service; others, on the contrary, fought tooth and nail against such worldly, even satanic, encroachments. It goes without saying that Rome itself neither sanctioned nor recognized the new songs.

Rome's authority in the early period, however, by

The Saviour Christ the Lord, the Child wrapped in swaddling clothes according to the message of the angels.

Here is the little one with Mary his Mother, of whom the prophet Isaiah foretold: Behold a Virgin shall conceive and bear a son. Now go and say that He is born.

Alleluia. We know already that Christ is born on the earth of whom you all must sing with the prophet saying: a Child is born.

18. See H. Reich, *op. cit.*, p. 105 seq.; also G. van der Leeuw, *Wegen—*, p. 136.

no means exacted the same strict obedience as the
Roman Catholic Church today. In those days, the
Church of Western Europe was full of disunity, strife,
uncertainty on points other than this one—too much
of this, indeed, was displayed to the population, Chris-
tianized only shortly before and at that often super-
ficially. It was not surprising, then, that Charlemagne
took such great interest in the sources of ecclesiastical
difference and disturbance. In the Council of Aix-la-
Chapelle, in 798, he worked towards a strict Church-
order to secure uniformity, correct liturgical language, and fix forever unity of ritual and conventions
of singing. For the same reason, Charlemagne labored
long and successfully for the installation of the Gregorian Mass order,[19] and brought the master-singers
Pierre and Romaine from Italy to the North to set a
standard for church singing. Romaine was sent to St.
Gall, where in all probability he initiated the vocalizations later so troublesome to Notker.[20]

At any rate, the Council of Aix-la-Chapelle ended
the fight over lay-songs: from then on, everything
sung in the Church had to be conceived in good
Church-Latin, which concentrated the renovations in
the hands of the clergy.[21] Laymen—the mass of the
faithful—were thus deprived of any influence on the
form and character of the divine service through the
introduction of their own hymns and liturgical addi-
tions. The composition of these innovations remained
from now on the privilege of that very small group in
the clergy which had a perfect command of Latin.
Whatever additions were made were hothouse plants,
cultivated in intellectual seclusion.

19. See O. Cargill, *op. cit.*, p. 11.
20. Gautier, *op. cit.*, p. 13 seq.
21. See H. F. Muller, "Pre-history of the Mediaeval Drama:
the Antecedents of the Tropes and the Conditions of their
Appearance," *Zeitschrift für Romanische Philologie,* 1924, p.
544 seq.

In the period which followed this establishment, it was the monks who labored diligently at this task, and it is almost exclusively their responsibility that tropes rose and flourished in this period in a movement spreading from monastery to monastery, remaining for the time being within the cloister walls. Of the fifty troparia, for instance, which Gautier investigated, only two or three were not of monastic origin, and they belonged to a period later than the eighth century.

Because of the emphasis upon good Church-Latin, writing tropes became a kind of exercise in style for the monks and their pupils.[22] Most of the texts are worse than mediocre. Understandably enough, it was fairly easy to smuggle such interpolations into divine service in the chapel of the monastery itself. "Quelques églises les ont admis," says Gautier, "l'Eglise non pas." [23] Some few were later incorporated at Rome into the reformed missal of Pius V, among them the moving sequence *Victimae Paschales Laudes*, probably created by the imperial chaplain Wipo in the eleventh century.[24]

By that time the flowering begun at St. Gall and later chiefly concentrated at St. Martial at Limoges was almost at an end. Soon after 1070 rhyme began to appear in France in tropes, which up to then had been exclusively rhythmical and written chiefly in hexameters. The result of this was that the interpolations were now prolonged: poetic talent was rarely revealed in these tropes, naturally enough, considering their origin. Prolongation,[25] however, proved fateful, for the long drawn-out songs thus introduced had

22. Gautier, *op. cit.*, p. 73 seq.
23. *Ibidem*, p. 138.
24. *Ibidem*, p. 7.
25. Cargill devotes a great part of his discussion to this period and believes that he can prove influence of the troubadours here.

neither pith nor marrow, and when worldly and satiri-
cal elements, even obscene expressions, were inserted
to hold the audience's attention, complete degeneration set in.

This can certainly be laid at the door of the *clerici
vagantes*, the Goliards,[26] who managed to enter the
monasteries for board and lodging on their wanderings by announcing at the gate that they had beauti-
ful new tropes. Once inside, they sang them. In 1227
the Council of Trier issued sharp warning against such
sinful practices, which took place long after the time
in which drama was born from ecclesiastical liturgy.

What was the precise order of events in this birth?
We must concentrate upon the tropes added to the
Christmas, Easter, Ascension, and Whitsun liturgies.
The Introit of the Mass was particularly subject to
interpolation, as we have seen in the case of Tutilo.
The Introit consists of four parts—the *Antiphona*,
"Nos autem gloriari aportet in Cruce Domini"; the
Psalmus, "Deus misereatur nostri et benedicat nobis";
the *Doxologia*, "Gloria Patri et Filio," and finally a
repetition of the *Antiphona*. All four parts had inter-
polations, in particular the final part preceding the
Mass.

The oldest insertion is the trope *Hodie cantandus*
in the Christmas liturgy, especially common in Germany. It was not the Christmas trope, however, but
the interpolation of the Easter Introit from which real
drama developed. The oldest St. Gall manuscript gives
it in this form:[27]

> *Quem quaeritis in sepulchro, o Christicolae?*
> *Jesum Nazarenum crucifixum, o coelicolae.*
> *Non est hic: Surrexit, sicut praedixerat.*
> *Ite, nuntiate quia surrexit de sepulchro.*

26. See Edmond Faral, *Les Jongleurs en France au Moyen
Age*, Paris, 1910, p. 32 seq.
27. Gautier, *op. cit.*, p. 220. Comp. K. Young, *op. cit.*. ch. IX,
"The Visit to the Sepulchre: first stage."

This is immediately followed by the *Resurrexi* of the official liturgy.

Just like the Christmas trope, this trope was soon prolonged, especially at St. Martial. Just as the Christmas trope was sung at the end of the procession to the altar where the manger was established, this dialogue was sung at Easter by the open tomb in which the cross and host had been laid at the *Depositio*. A careful comparing makes it clear that the Easter-trope, so generally considered the seed of modern drama, is in itself no whit more dramatic than the interpolations into other festivals of the Church. There is for the celebrants here no more incentive to impersonation of the angel and the women than there is urge for portrayal of the shepherds in the Christmas trope. Nor did Young deny this.[28]

But the fact is that the Easter drama developed much earlier and more extensively than the Church play put on at the other holy festivals. The solution to this problem Young found in the fact that at a certain point the Easter trope was removed from the Introit, set ahead, and connected with the Matins. This change was unquestionably of great importance, for it gave the trope opportunity to expand which it had not had in its old strictly limited position as part of the Introit, directly before the beginning of Mass, where all attention must be concentrated. When the trope was transferred to the end of the Matins, it came between the last Response and the concluding *Te Deum*. No climax followed it; the jubilation of the final hymn could be postponed and the trope had sufficient time and place to develop.

It was also a fortunate coincidence—which may have motivated the transfer—that the little dialogue between the angel and the women was then sung at daybreak, the moment the Matins were supposed to

28. K. Young, *op. cit.*, I, p. 110.

end. It took place, therefore, on Easter morning itself, the very day referred to by the trope. Amalarius of Metz, that advocate of representation, must have applauded this change. When it took place is not known, though Young assures us that "in the Visitatio impersonation became customary as early as the latter half of the tenth century." [29]

This statement, of course, needs further clarification, which he does not give. Although no medievalist has studied this material with Young's thoroughness, here he falls below his own standard and makes a statement without giving motives and evidence, though we may assume that Ethelwold's report is his only source. We must know the *cause* of impersonation in this trope, for before its shift in position there had been no impersonation in any of the tropes or in any other part of the official liturgy.

Such a transformation is no small matter, for the celebrant's representation in the divine service never aims at and never achieves even apparent identification with the character for which he stands. It was thus possible for him to join in the singing of the *Te Deum* with which the trope concluded, for he could not drop out of a "role" where no role existed.

How far apart this is in essence and appearance from portrayal, which seeks by imitation to recreate an original, at least in outward form. Not even the similarity for which the celebrant strove in the liturgy can bridge the gap between symbolic action in the divine service, of which the essentials are idea and commemoration, and action which portrays the very life portrayed. For the transition, for the inner metamorphosis of such essential importance in the development of drama, not even Young, who can never be accused of mere philology, can give a reason: he can only say that it came to pass when the Easter trope

29. *Ibidem*, I, p. 238.

was transferred from the Introit to the end of the
Matins and there had opportunity to expand. Must we
then understand that it was space, merely space and
growth, which changed the celebrant into an actor
and delivered theater from religion?

Then why did that theater not rise from other
dialogues of the liturgy, from the Mass itself, which,
too, through the ages had undergone the process of
expansion? Would it not have been highly preferable
for dramatic art to have originated in the official service, not in the illegitimate contraband of the tropes?
And, more seriously, what other religion among those
analogies and parallels used to prove the birth of the
theater in the medieval Church was "génératrice de
drame" solely through the extension of ritual symbolic action?

This question takes us back to the research into
the birth of theater from the rites of primitives and
ancients. We concluded the previous chapter with
a summary of the earmarks and characteristics which
led in both cases to the origin of drama. What comparison is there between them and the theatrogenetic
element in the liturgy, the trope? What comparison
is there with the Christian Church itself?

We found in primitive and ancient rites first a mass
movement in which everyone could participate and
which led to a common ecstasy. With the tropes we
are confined within the monastery walls where men
lived in seclusion and meditation. There was of course
joy among them on the feast-days of the Church, as
the *Eia et eia* resounding in their tropes bear witness;
they experienced deep and holy emotion when at the
end of the Easter Matins the *Quem quaeritis* began
and the message of the Resurrection was heard. But
how far removed was the essence of their joy and
emotion from the ecstasy of the primitives, which
breaking all bounds found its form only in frenetic
dance!

The monks celebrated a commemoration, celebrated through the entire Christian Church by symbolism and never in the world can symbolism belie its cerebral origin. Although Western Europe in the later Middle Ages knew expressions of mass-ecstasy, they were never the result of emotion evoked by the liturgy as such; it was, indeed, the cerebral center of liturgy that kept the emotions it engendered far from the frantic ecstasy of the primitives and the Greeks. This difference is particularly important for the enclosure of the cloister chapels, where we find the tropes and their fullest extension.

Archaic peoples aimed not at commemoration, but at action, to which they brought all the force and passion they had to become one with the Power, with the Invisible. As we saw, this communion was not granted the cultist and Maenad from above, but was wrested from the deity: man conquered the god. Could there possibly be a sharper and deeper contrast between this practice and the lessons of Christianity?

In Christianity it is not man who in common with other men and by his own force reaches God and participates in Him, but God who bestows his Grace on man, and on man as an individual. In Christ's words, "My Grace is sufficient for thee," lies the core of the Gospel. All Christians praise and exult in God's Grace, but what has their exaltation to do with the *ecstasis* and *enthousiasmos* of the heathen worshipper, flung out of himself by his wild dance, feeling God, united with God, portraying him with his own body? The presence of the mask corroborates this identification.

For primitive and ancient religions and the theater that arose from them, in the beginning was the deed, and the deed was with man, and the deed was man, Christianity replaced this with "In the beginning was the Word, and the Word was with God, and the Word was God." The fundamental opposition of these two concepts leads us to believe that it is impos-

sible for the Christian Church in any century or period to have created drama in a way analogous to
primitive and ancient rites. Cohen's law does not hold
for Christianity.

Though we have already drawn our conclusion, we
will test Christianity for another quality found in
archaic rite. The force behind primitive worship and
the Dionysus cult appears to have been the lust for
life, the sharp desire for eternal continuity in this
earthly existence. On this score, too, the contrast of
primitive with Christian belief cannot be more pronounced.

This is a point of pre-eminent importance. It is the
essence of dramatic art always to be the showpiece of
the world, the reflection of its outer as well as its inner
conflicts. It can never reach above or beyond life and
death. Can a religion which looks through life and
above it longing for fulfillment of the Kingdom of
Heaven, can a church which "has almost replaced
good and evil by the bodily and the non-bodily" [30]
spontaneously and willingly resurrect an art which
exists by the grace of earthly life and may not pass
its boundaries? Nowhere is the answer better given
than at the end of that most spiritual of plays, *Every-
man*.

For the second time the parallels drawn to affirm
the clerical birth of drama have proved the exact opposite. Once more it is evident that Cohen's law does
not hold for Christianity and the Christian Church.

Let us make one thing clear: this examination is
directed exclusively at the origin of theater. When
definite dramatic forms have been established, a
church, no matter how opposed it might have been to
theater, may see some desirability in employing that
theater and even in participating directly in its further
development. This is precisely what took place in the

30. G. van der Leeuw, *Wegen*—, p. 69.

Church between the tenth and thirteenth centuries. In the same way, perhaps, the opposition between symbolism and action was bridged in a later phase—a much later phase in the intellectual development of society—when the metaphorical symbol of play and the life-image of the theater were brought together in the moralities. Such encounters are mostly brief, because of intrinsic opposition; for this reason the ties of the theater to the Christian Church are inevitably of a temporary nature. Pope Innocent III's ban in 1207 was by no means the first resistance of clerical authority to this tie in the Middle Ages.

And despite this, the theater flourished in the Church. The first writings in which we find dramatic activities mentioned, after a silence of several centuries, set the theater in the Church. There, under the Church's supervision, the development began which led to the great mystery plays of the fifteenth century.

We are still left with a question. If, as we have tried to prove, the origin of theater does not lie in the Church, then where did dramatic art come from? Why did the Church abandon its ancient enmity and adopt this art in the ninth and tenth centuries?

5: *The Mime*

It was not out of opposition to its essential nature and purpose alone that the Church condemned the theater. It feared the destruction of the actor's and the spectator's soul, the pagan temptation of theater which caused the fathers of the church to regard it as Satan's tool.

The theater aroused indignation and scorn, and the militant clergy made no attempt to hide their animosity. Even the most tolerant Christian could not really accept theatrical representations of the bishops as grotesque ithyphallic characters and of the sacrament of baptism[1] as a dunking-party in a tub, from which the fool was finally fished up a baptized Christian. How the spacious Roman amphitheaters with their thousands of spectators must have rocked with laughter at the comic rites of a silly Nazarene sect.

Very early, Christian apologists responded with curses to a theater that did not scruple to ridicule their holiest institutions. With the growth of the Church's power, the bitterness of its attack increased, and the theater no doubt became more circumspect in its expression. Chrysostom found sufficient cause, nevertheless, to dedicate a great part of his life to combating this indecent enemy, though he had little reason to be proud of the results of his endeavors.

The Roman stage was ruled by the mime, who presented an extremely varied art, both in the time of the emperors and before it. In the Greek theater, too, his domination had been virtually unlimited, for the Golden Age of tragedy and comedy had not, after

1. II. Reich, *op. cit.*, p. 80-141. *Ibidem*, p. 182 seq.

all, lasted long. All over the ancient world these comedians, cittern-players, clowns, dancers, and prestidigitators grouped under the name of *Mimes* had made an increasing claim upon the theater. Their appearance, which began as an *intermezzo,* ended as the main event. Their portrayal of life mirrored its unlimited variations: their realistic plays, full of jokes, gaiety, satire, and the necessary tears packed the enormous Mediterranean theaters and kept them resounding with cheers for ten centuries.

The *mimesis biou* (portrayal of life) was the task of a theater unlimited in its form and expression by literary or national laws. The mime required freedom and without it could not portray life as he saw it: i.e., as he exposed, ridiculed, burlesqued, mourned, or glorified it. Because he attacked or praised life in the manner his audiences wished to hear, he was certain of mass protection, and only rarely do we hear of despots and tyrannical emperors who dared defy the people and the mimes.[2]

From fifth-century Greece, where the mime is first mentioned, to the end of his trail in the collapsing Roman World, the mime is a typical professional and versatile artist. Whether he does a tightrope act, juggles, or plays the fool, the mime is above all an actor, singer, dancer—and that simultaneously; from his art derive the expressions *cantare tragediam* and *saltare tragediam.* His tragedy had little to do with that of Sophocles and the other Athenian poets, but in all probability various classical works performed the same function for the mime as Goethe's *Faust* for Gounod.

As an entertainer, the mime had other employments than the ones named, and in the ancient world all these had different names. The word *mime* was understood to cover them all, but indicated primarily the singer-actor. His counterpart is also found in the

2. A. Nicoll, *op. cit. passim,* o.a. p. 17.

Greek *Phlyakes*,[3] the Latin *Atellans*, and in many other kinds of folk theater. His types still exist in modern European farce, not only as traditional heritage, but because their comment on life is simple and apt; in their shows criticism of that life finds a tangible form, which is readily appreciated and often long remembered.

Freedom was the mime's privilege and so long as it was granted him, he made good use of it; his portrayals of life knew no taboos and for this reason many called them scandalous. Seneca came to the mime's defense in his statement that "our times are so full of unbelievable vices that the mimes could sooner be accused of dereliction of duty." [4] The pagan priest hated the mimes as much as the early Church father, but for the multitude's applause and cheers the mimes were willing to risk much. Their own and alien gods functioned as clowns and fools in their burlesques; why should they not poke fun at Christian rites, which appeared to them and their public both silly and incomprehensible?

When after some time, the balance began to shift in favor of Christianity, mimic satire gradually changed in emphasis and subject; no more farces took place around the baptismal tub. Enough remained to be scoffed at: for instance, the never-ending wrangles over dogma and the mutual vindictiveness of the various groups and sects within the Church. What annoyed the leaders of the Church most deeply was the resounding applause which the incorrigible mime received from his Christian public.

That the mimes managed to retain their traditional popularity appears from the Council of Nicea in 325,

3. The vases form our main source.
4. Seneca, *De Brevitate Vitae*, 12, 13: "Plura mehercules praetereunt quam fingent et tanta incredibilium vitiorum copia ingenioso in hoc saeculo processit, ut iam mimorum arguere possis neglegentiam."

when St. Athanasius not unreasonably accused Arius of wanting to smuggle into the Church service the mimes' popular songs.[5] Later in the same century, St. Gregory Nazianzen also vehemently attacked the Arian heresy; nevertheless, he laid the foundation of Christian song[6] with his Virgin's Song and Vesper Song, borrowed from the theater and adapted the meter from a mimic stanza. Perhaps this merely serves to clarify his bitter attacks upon the mimes.

Gregory was certainly not alone in his attack, but he could not count upon the support of the entire Church, for many princes of the Church followed the Roman and Byzantine emperors in openly admitting their warm appreciation of the mimes. Though Church leaders like Chrysostom raged and threatened the congregation with excommunication as punishment for attendance at the theater, what effect could this have when the great in church and state set such an example? To what height did the reputation of the mime not rise when the Emperor Justinian raised one of them to share his throne as the Empress Theodora? Yet he dared later to issue a ban on the theater which for a time prohibited it. But the profession survived both his glorification and his banishment without much trouble.

The bishops might forbid the theater in their solemn conclave of 692, but it is well known that in the same Byzantium that was host to the Trullan Council, the condemned not only did fairly well, but even prospered. Moreover, they continued to prosper in the place of honor consistently accorded the mimes, at the Court of the Byzantine emperors, up to the time of the Paleologi.[7] Bishop Liutprand of Cremona,[8]

5. H. Reich, *op. cit.*, p. 140.
6. See G. van der Leeuw, *Wegen—*, p. 136.
7. H. Reich, *op. cit.*, p. 202.
8. See K. Krumbacher, *Geschichte der byzantinischen Literatur von Justinianus bis zum Ende des Oströmischen Reiches* (Handb. Klass. Alt.) München, 1897.

twice sent as ambassador to Constantinople by the
Emperor Otto about 970, complained that Hagia
Sophia had been turned into a theater—but he considered an explanation of the word "theater" superfluous for his western readers. Other western travelers
to the Eastern Empire did not comment on the theaters, which indicates that they were not unfamiliar
with such institutions.

During the empire, the mimes pushed their way
into the provinces, and after the fall of Rome, they
disappeared no less there than in the centers of civilization. The theaters themselves declined and fell into
ruin,[9] and with them disappeared the last vestiges of
classical tragedy and comedy. This did not undo the
mimes, however, for from the time of the *Phlyakes*
they had been accustomed to a temporary structure
in the enormous amphitheaters[10] and to the *siparium*
(small curtain) on the big *scena*, from behind which
they emerged for their numbers and acts.[11] When
Isidore of Seville wrote his great encyclopedia in the
seventh century,[12] he mentioned the theater as a thing
of the past but described the mimes and their activities in the present tense.

They may have worked in combination with the
Gallic bard [13] in Western Europe, and a relation between them and the scop is quite probable. At any
rate, the mime seems to have lost little if any of his
ancient character; all occupations from prestidigitator
to dancer, from singer-actor to puppet-master and

9. On theaters in a later period see Roger S. Loomis, "Were
there Theatres in the Twelfth and Thirteenth Centuries?"
with comm. by Gustave Cohen, *Speculum*, 1945, XX, 1; under
the same title denied by Dino Bigongiari in *Romantic Review,*
Oct. 1946.
10. See M. Bieber, *op. cit.*, ch. X.
11. A. Nicoll, *op. cit.*, p. 105 seq.
12. Isidorus, *Etymologiae seu origines,* ed. M. Lindsay, Oxford,
1911.
13. Faral, *op. cit.*, p. 4.

teller of tales accompanying himself on the *vielle* were considered as belonging to the same profession.[14] Their motley garb, from which the fool's costume originated, belonged to the same wardrobe as the *centuculus* of the ancient mime.[15] The old names, *histrio, mimus, joculator, saltator*, and others, persisted until late into the Middle Ages.[16]

This very diversity sometimes brought confusion and annoyance, especially among the major and minor stars, in the hierarchical world of artists. In the thirteenth century, Guiraut Riquier,[17] who as Provençal *Contrafazedor* felt the troubadour's pride, requested Alfonso the Wise to appoint titles and grades for the different kinds of jongleurs—a request the good Castilian king granted. As Guiraut had expected, the composers of serious poetry were placed at the top. Somewhat earlier, Thomas de Cabham[18] had made a similar division along moral lines, though he made a few technical distinctions—those who used masks, those who accompanied themselves on musical instruments, those whose program apparently best satisfied the great lords, etc.

Nevertheless, it is extremely difficult for us to distinguish within this great group, which in spite of all differences, has maintained its solidarity up to the present, so that even today a leading actor in the legitimate theater feels kinship with the clown of the traveling circus and—to the amazement of the bourgeois—is not ashamed of that relationship. Interest-

14. *Ibidem*, p. 5; Chambers, *The Med. Stage*, I, p. 23 seq.
15. A. Nicoll, *op. cit.*, p. 91; H. Reich, *op. cit.*, p. 797.
16. On *Comedia Bile* see E. Beutler, "Die *Comedia Bile*, ein antiker Mimus bei den Gauklern des 15 Jahrhunderts," *Germ. Rom. Monatschr*. XIV, 1926, p. 81 seq.
17. Creizenach, *op. cit.*, I, p. 38; Chambers, *The Med. Stage*, I, p. 63; Joseph Anglade, *Le troubadour Guiraut Riquier; Etude sur la décadence de l'ancienne poésie provençale*, diss. Un. d. Paris, 1905 (Bordeaux), p. 122 seq.
18. See page 2; comp. A. Nicoll, *op. cit.*, p. 152 seq.

ingly enough, Nicoll emphatically pointed out that in the Middle Ages, the designations *histrio* and *joculator* were frequently connected with the word *scenicus*, from which it appears that all these names were inextricably bound up with the idea of "performance."

It goes without saying that in the West the Church's rage inevitably pursued the mime. St. Jerome had made an early start, armed with all the force of his rhetoric, and throughout the Middle Ages councils and synods expressed themselves with particular vehemence against the mime under all his names. It proves that far from being dead the mime was doing quite well. What is peculiarly striking about these decrees is that over and over again Church authorities address themselves to the clergy and exhort them to keep their distance from the dangerous mimes. The repetition of this reproof indicates an association, perhaps even a friendship which could not otherwise have been deduced from contemporary manuscripts.

At the court of Charlemagne, the strict and rigid Alcuin did all he could as counselor to the Emperor to oppose the love for the mime which his spiritual brother and colleague, Angilbert, the Homer of the court,[19] felt. In 813 the Synod of Tours bade the clergy keep away from mimes, and in the same year the Synod of Châlons and the Council of Mainz issued the same edict. The associations between clergy and mimes must have been frequent and close.

These orders did not do much good, for in 816 the Council of Aix-la-Chapelle forbade the clergy to be present at any performance, and in 829 the Council of Paris accused the priests of neglecting their duty for the entertainment of the mimes. In 847 the Council of Mainz repeated the command as did the Council of Nantes in 890, in which there was further mention of mimes using *larves daemonum*, devils'

19. H. Alt, *Theater und Kirche*, p. 401: H. Reich, *op. cit.*, p. 793.

masks.[20] Agobert, Archbishop of Lyons,[21] in 836 re-
buked the faithless prelates and clergymen who,
according to his strictures, wasted the Church's prop-
erty on mimes, meanwhile allowing the poor to die
of starvation. Alcuin had levelled a similar accusation
at the English bishop Higbald, urging him to feed the
poor rather than the *histriones*.

In the ninth century the frequency of these com-
plaints is remarkable. We must mention in this connection a ruling from Charlemagne's *Capitularia* by
which the clergy—bishops, abbots, and abbesses mentioned by name—were forbidden to own hunting
dogs, falcons, hawks, and *joculatores*. Another para-
graph threatened with corporal punishment anyone
who "ex scenicis" dressed himself in priestly or monastic garb.[22]

From this passage Nicoll concluded two possibilities; either the mime attempted to ridicule the clergy
as he had always done, or the mime had become chris-
tianized and gave performances of Christian subjects
and of religious nature. I do not believe that the former conclusion can be correct. We have already
noted Charlemagne's efforts to purify the Church and
thus to maintain its power. Under his rule, ridicule
would have received much sharper measures than corporal punishment and banishment—far likelier per-
secution and annihilation. The mime had always had
to avoid such open conflicts, and in view of the active
and extensive patronage he enjoyed, indicated by the
conciliar and synodal decrees, it is unacceptable that
he would venture to ridicule the clergy, as this would
have caused his benefactors to give earlier obedience
to the Councils.

20. A. Nicoll, *op. cit.*, p. 147 seq.
21. H. Reich, *op. cit.*, p. 795.
22. *Caroli Magni Capitularia*, ed. Heineccius, vol. V, p. 150 seq.:
"Si quis ex scenicis vestem sacerdotalem aut monasticum vel
mulieris religiosae, vel qualicumque ecclesiastico statu similem
indutus fuerit, corporali poena subsistat et exilio tradatur."

Thus the only possibility remaining is that the mimes gave religious performances—a particularly far-reaching conclusion, which, for the present at least, I shall not use as a foundation to build upon. It is Nicoll's "either-or" which has led to this conclusion, though I must add that I see no possibility of a third explanation.[23] If the Emperor were aiming at the performance of religious plays, it is strange that his proclamations were directed only against the actors and did not forbid the clergy to lend their vestments. In the matter of costume, cooperation between actors and clergy was indispensable.

An entirely different interpretation of the connection between the two groups can be given by questioning whether the words *histrio* and *mimus* meant more than *citharista*. In his letter to Higbald, Alcuin mentioned the two first names, but by no means in the same breath; his sentence structure makes it clear that he had two kinds of parasites in mind. It is difficult to see why the Church should warn so strongly against self-accompanying singers and tellers of tales: no, it was portrayal, the imitation of life, from the first century A.D. felt to be a devil's invention and condemned as a destructive influence. No one bothered about recitation and singing.

The glosses, moreover, point in the direction of the stage: *scenicus* and *mimus* mean the same thing, as does *histrio* also. In a Vatican codex *scena* is paraphrased as *theatri locus aut ludus mimicus*, "the place of the theater or the mimic play." [24] In 1215 the Lateran Council spoke of *mimis, joculatoribus et histrionibus* in one breath.[25] The name *joculator* or *jongleur* is a later addition to the other two names, and

23. If we assume as third possibility that the mimes represented clergy in secular plays without ridiculing them, then it is hard to see how such activities could cause the scorn of the Emperor.
24. A. Nicoll, *op. cit.*, p. 151.
25. Chambers, *The Med*. Stage, I, 32, note.

appears no earlier than the ninth century.[26] Though the name throughout Europe—*Gaukler*, *goochelaar*, *juggler*—points to a many-sided activity, nonetheless the word frequently indicated the same thing as *mimus* and *histrio*.

This is also made clear by Hugutius, who about 1200 explained to his contemporaries in his *Liber Derivationum*[27] how the plays of Terence were performed in the old days. Naturally enough, he followed the medieval misconception of the narrator, Calliopius; he described those who acted out the recitation as *mimi joculatores*, terms which apparently gave his readers a clear picture of their activities. The same *joculatores* served to describe the masked actors in the famous miniatures in the Terence manuscripts in the Bibliothèque de l'Arsenal and the Bibliothèque Nationale in Paris.[28]

This should provide sufficient evidence that the words *histrio* and *mimus* did not describe musicians, but actors, against whom the Church Councils hurled their proclamations, actors who resembled in many ways the opera singers and ballet dancers of our day. For all of them, physical portrayal was the basis of their art; in this lies their essential difference from the *citharista*, the singer of songs and teller of tales.

The century in which the Church issued its anti-mimic edicts was the one in which the trope came into fashion. When we realize that from earliest times the musical element was essential in the productions of the mime, we recognize another cause of the *histriones'* attraction for the clergy. For the first time

26. Faral, *op. cit.*, p. 2 seq. and p. 11 seq.
27. Max Hermann, *Forschungen*—, ch. "Dramenillustrationen des 15 und 16 Jahrh." Hermann copied (p. 287) from the Berlin ms.: "mimus ioculator et proprie reum humanarum imitator, sicut olim erant in recitatione comediarum, quia quod verbo recitator dicebat mimi motu corporis exprimebant."
28. A. Nicoll, *op. cit.*, *fig.* 102 and 103. See Creizenach, *op. cit.*, I, p. 4 seq. and G. Cohen, *La Comedie latine*—

the development of the trope into drama is put into
a different—and this time proper—perspective. The
tropes, as we have seen, were the product of monasteries. The synodal and conciliar proclamations directed against the mimes never name the monasteries
specifically, either because hierarchical correctness ad-
dressed only the higher and supervising clergy, or
because the Councils did not regard the monasteries
as guilty in this matter. The latter explanation seems
unlikely in view of the fact that in the proclamation
of the Capitularia, specific abbots and abbesses were
named.

There is still another and quite conclusive evidence
of connection between monasteries and mimes in the
matter of tropes. We have already said that the center
of trope-cultivation shifted from St. Gall even before
the tenth century to the abbey of St. Martial at Limoges, the abbey which led Western Europe in the
production and development of tropes. From this
monastery exists a troparium, now in the Bibliothèque
Nationale in Paris, richly illuminated with miniatures[29] as many of these trope-books are. In it I found
miniatures of great importance, for they portray the
various mimes in their performances—acting, dancing,
accompanying themselves on musical instruments. Especially pages 109 and 114, here reproduced, seem
highly interesting.

What business have these enemies of the Church in
a collection of monastic songs? They are certainly not
simply decorative, like the elephant and other decorations around the text.[30] Moreover, the actors are so
vividly and realistically depicted that we must assume
the miniatures to be portraits: the only conclusion we
can draw is that the artist considered the pictures of
mimes to belong to the *cantilenae*. He must have seen

29. Bibl. Nat. Lat. 1118, Fo 109 r°, 113 v°, 114 r°.
30. Occasionally miniaturists might insert illustrations not related to the text; it happened, however, very rarely.

them acting, dancing, singing in the very tropes he illustrated. Certainly, nothing could better serve as illumination of the text here than the direct illustration, the portrayal of that performance.

The importance of these miniatures is that they are indisputable. Merely from the meaning of the words *histrio, mimus, joculator* one could never arrive at better than half-certainty. No scribe of the tenth century dared take the liberty to devote more than a disapproving and therefore incidental reference to the despised worldlings in a pious book, and copyists had as little temptation to make digressions. But the miniaturist occupied an entirely different position: from other manuscripts as well, we know that he enjoyed far greater liberty; and in this case, he had a chance to describe exactly what he had seen. From his evidence we can see that the mimes of his day were little changed from those of antiquity, and—what is far more important for us—that they were closely connected with the tropes. He immortalized neither priests nor clerics, but mimes in his troparium; would he have done so, if they had not been the tropes' performers?

This fact throws some light upon the all too dim stage of the medieval theater. If the mimes were called in to perform the tropes, it immediately becomes clear how the element of impersonation was introduced, for instance, into the Easter trope. It was not merely space—as Young made us conjecture—and opportunity for expansion which introduced a completely anomalous element and effected the transition from symbolic liturgy into theater; it was the mimes, traditionally unable to limit themselves to cerebral presentation, who endowed the ceremony with the actual life which was their professional concern. The dialogue as they sang it was thus no longer a commemorative recital, but an occasion for mimic portrayal and recreation of an event from the past. Naturally, their performance was not comparable to acting in a modern theater: it took place in a church, reason enough why complete realism could not be their aim. But it *was* a play, no longer symbolism—that was the critical change.

Quite aside from the evidence of these miniatures of St. Martial, the use of mimes in the divine service is not incomprehensible and unacceptable; the Church has always, with wisdom and discretion, adopted and sanctified worldly elements from which the people, the congregation, would not willingly be parted. When we see that even the clergy could not or would not suppress their love for the mimes, we need no further evidence of their popularity. How could the Church have shown greater wisdom than to make their art serviceable to its aims and thus to remove the satanic temptation it implied?

In the eighth century, John of Damascus[31] had attacked the mob's veneration of the mime and compared their lewd performances with the solemn spectacle of the Mass. Though his words showed little awareness of the nature of the liturgy, he clearly expressed the idea of competition between the liturgy and mimic performance, particularly in his rebuke to those who spent all day in the theaters and left no time for church. A foe is never so effectively beaten as with his own weapons and strategy, as the Church well knew. We shall have occasion to discuss this policy of the Church more extensively.

We must also take into consideration that the same aestheticism prevailed in the monasteries that we recognize in clerical art-patronage of the Renaissance. It is certainly possible that the clerical leaders in twelfth-century cultural centers preferred to see their literary and musical creations performed by professionals who understood their artistic purpose than by

31. A. Nicoll, *op. cit.*, p. 147.

pupils in monastic schools—for even at St. Gall Notker had difficulty with the artistic talents of his pupils.[32] Worldly artists made their way into the monasteries for less exalted reasons too: minstrels were
sometimes hired to compose and sing *chansons de
geste* in an effort to attract pilgrims to particular relics
and sanctuaries,[33] and we may assume that the minstrels did not limit themselves to that once they were
within the cloister walls. This fact clarifies how much
importance must have been attached to good and
inviting performances of the tropes.

It has long been established[34] that later in the
eleventh and twelfth centuries the ordinary clergy
also made regular use of the services of the mimes in
various places in Western Europe and in different
ways. Faral records the significant fact that in Abbé-
ville the church itself was put at the players' disposal
for the performances of farces on Lady-day. On that
holiday, the priest had the title of "roi des ribauds,"
with jurisdiction over the players; after 1291, this latter right reverted to the city.[35]

But of all this evidence the miniatures of St. Martial
speak most clearly. They help explain how drama
sprang from the tropes—or rather, how the tropes
developed into drama. The professional player was
forced, because of his particular creative talents, to pro-
duce a new drama which for some time afterward developed under the supervision of the Church.

In the meantime, the old, ordinary craft of the
mimes continued to exist: their romantic pageants,
their farces, their sketches and songs, in short, their

32. J. Handschin, "Über Estampie und Sequenz," *Zeitschrift
fur Musikwissensch.*, XII, 1, is of the opinion that the sequence
"aus der Spielmannskunst gespeist wurde." Hans J. Moser in
Geschichte der deutschen Musik, Stuttgart, 1930, I, also points
to influences from outside the Church.
33. J. Bedier, *Les légendes épiques*, Paris, 1908.
34. Faral, *op. cit.*, p. 31 and ch. III.
35. *Ibidem*, p. 88.

secular theater continued just as it had in the past and provided valuable stimulus to the development of religious theater. First of all, it provided some competition, which in their own defense led the clergy to cooperate with the mimes and to develop theatrical attractions for the congregation. It remained necessary to pull the mass away from the satanic entertainment, which it so greedily enjoyed. Thus the Easter play began to expand, helped by the mimes.

One would expect the Passion play soon to be taken up in this expansion: a more moving drama than that of the suffering Christ can hardly be imagined, especially for the medieval public, united in one faith and one Church. The tremendous impression the Passion created in the later mystery plays is thoroughly attested. It is singular that before the beginning of the thirteenth century, there is no mention whatever of a dramatized Passion. With material of this kind, there is no question of a hidden play scribes might have considered unfit to be recorded. No, the fact is quite clear: the Church play at the end of Holy Week for centuries ignored the Passion completely and limited itself to the scenes at the sepulchre and the resurrection.[36]

The first interpolations between the traditional scenes of grief and joy occurred in Germany: the apostles' racing and the bargaining of the Holy Women with the unguent merchant.[37] The performing mimes did not let this opportunity to display their comic talents pass unused—for every tragedian seizes the chance to show off his *vis comica*—indeed, they may even have added these scenes themselves.

Clerical supervisors would not have opposed the addition of comic scenes, for they increased the attractiveness of Church-plays, making them a more effective weapon against the worldly mime. In the

36. K. Young, *op. cit.*, I, p. 402.
37. H. H. Borcherdt, *Das Europaische Theater—*, p. 35.

Christmas plays similar developments began to take place. Here it was especially the scenes of the raging Herod which gave comic relief. The clergy, however, retained the leadership and was careful to draw the line against too great profanity wherever necessary. The complaint made about 1150 by Herrad of Landsberg, Abbess of Hohenburg, who could not restrain her annoyance at these slapstick scenes, indicates that the line was not always drawn satisfactorily; still others agreed with Gerhof of Reichersberg[38] that all *spectacula theatrica* were plain devil's work and desecrated the church.

In such plays as the Innsbruck Passion play and the Easter play of St. Gall considerable space was taken up by the comic parts of the congregating Jews, the good-for-nothing Rufus, and the picaresque Rubin;[39] in the eleventh and twelfth centuries, the humorous element became stronger and stronger. From this development the theory was enunciated that these scenes in ecclesiastical drama gave rise to the new comic theater.[40] Since the origin of Greek comedy had also been found in religion, the famous analogy with Greek theater was evoked. It should be quite clear by now that, even if one should consider such scenes in the Passion plays and Christmas plays the sources of later farce, it is impossible to speak of their religious origin. This element of humor is, like the whole theatrical character of the liturgical play, alien to Christian divine service and imported from outside it.

A religious explanation is, moreover, entirely superfluous, for the mimes continued to play their farces outside the Church. Scribes, of course, considered

38. Creizenach, *op. cit.*, I. p. 58 and p. 94.
39. *Ibidem*, p. 108 seq.
40. Maurice Wilmotte, "L'Elément comique dans le théâtre réligieux" in *Etudes sur la tradition littéraire en France*, Paris, 1909, p. 93 seq.
   Eugène Lintilhac, *Histoire générale du théâtre en France*, Paris, 1904-11, II, p. 21 seq.

only those plays worthy of perpetuating which had been performed in the Church, and not until the growth of vernacular literature did other scribes go to work on secular plays. One such man collected, in the so-called Hulthem Manuscript, various pieces of Netherlandish literature which appeared to him worth reading; by this chance, the *Abele spelen* were preserved, the oldest romantic dramas known to us, and with them, the *cluten* or farces.[41]

If we recall the various types of characters in these farces—Lippijn, he who is slapped; the old skirtchaser Buskenblaser; the shrewd quack and the bête Rubben—we can see parading before us the twin brothers of Stupidus and Sannio, Pappus the Parasite, and the Maccus of the Latin mimes and Atellans. Illustrations for these farce-types might be chosen from the Greek vases portraying the Phlyakes. Nicoll pointed out the similarity of the Herod of the Christmas-play, the *miles gloriosus*, and the later *Capitano* of the commedia dell'arte. And is not the Joseph of the mystery plays the Stupidus of earlier times and the Pantalone of later? We must look for the origin of the humorous *intermezzi* in liturgical drama where it belongs logically and psychologically—with the theater, among the mimes.

As for the secular drama of the Middle Ages, we have no need of analogy to the Greek tragedy. Nobody so far has bothered to doubt its liturgical origin —no matter what the origin of liturgical drama itself. Still it is useful to examine the pertinent material chronologically, and for once not to establish facts and developments in the ninth, tenth, and eleventh

41. Ed. P. Leendertz in *Middelnederlandsche Dramatische Poezie*, Leiden. See also Frank G. van der Riet, *Le théâtre profane sérieux en langue Flamande au moyen age*, La Haye, 1936. Transl. in English of the *Abele spel van Lanseloet* (Lancelot of Denmark) by P. Geyl. The Hague, 1923 and the *Abele spel of Esmoreit* by Harry Morgan Ayres. The Hague, 1923.

centuries by using manuscripts of the fifteenth, sixteenth, and later centuries, in order to construct a
"logical" sequence.[42]

The liturgical plays in their simplest Latin form
appear, without any notable change, from the tenth to
the sixteenth century. The oldest expansion extant is
a play of the Magi—really a Herod play, since the
portrayal of the wicked king completely overshadows
the adoration—in the manuscript of Nevers, and also
in those of Compiègne, Bilsen, and Freising. This play
dates from the eleventh century. In the twelfth century we find an expansion of the Easter play in the
Tours manuscript, followed chronologically by the
manuscripts of Benediktbeuer and Klosterneuburg in
the thirteenth century. Other twelfth-century plays
are the Play of the Anti-Christ from Tegernsee, the
Play of the Wise and Foolish Virgins from Angou-
lême, the Play of Lucifer—performed in Regensburg
in 1194 but of which no text survives—and two plays
of the Prophet Daniel, one by the Anglo-Norman
Hilarius,[43] the other by an unknown author from the
scholars' circle at Beauvais. These are the most important Latin Church-dramas known in this period.[44]

The oldest Church-play in the vernacular is the
Norman *Jeu d'Adam*, of about the year 1150. It was
followed about fifty years later by the *Jeu de St.
Nicolas*, by the Arras poet Jean Bodel. Bodel's work
hardly belongs to the category of clerical-liturgical
drama: if we compare it, for instance, to the Nether-

42. Karl Young followed this method; see his introduction
(*op. cit.*, VIII seq.) and, for instance, vol. I, p. 230 where he
has the tenth-century *Regularis Concordia* immediately followed by a *Visitatio* from eighteenth-century Angiers.

43. Cargill associates the degeneration of the tropes with the
appearance of the troubadours and pays much attention to
Hilarius (*op. cit.*, p. 43 seq.) whose works he cannot accept as
development in Church drama.

44. For other St. Nicolas plays see Creizenach, *op. cit.*, p. 97
seq.

landish *Gloriant*, it becomes increasingly doubtful
which is the secular and which the religious play.
Rutebeuf's short *Theophilus* on the other hand, a
miracle play of Our Lady written about 1200, is unquestionably a liturgical play. From thirteenth-century Germany, we have only fragments: the remains
of an Easter play from Muri and of a Low-German
Nativity play from the monastery Himmelgarten at
Nordhausen, both of the second half of the century.
If we stretch a point, we may include the half-Latin,
half-German play of Mary's Ascension. From England there are records of performances before 1200,
a Resurrection play put on at Beverly the text of
which has not been preserved, so that we cannot be
sure whether the play was written in Latin or in the
vernacular. From the mid-thirteenth century comes
a Harrowing of Hell only 244 lines long, the dramatic
character of which has quite properly been ques-
tioned.[45]

In the fourteenth century, too, the list is short: in
France, a *Jeu de l'Antichrist* and some Miracles of
Our Lady, which belong to this century though the
manuscripts are of a later date—and many of these
betray a secular lineage. There is an Easter play from
Provence, a second in German from Trier, a third
from Innsbruck; from St. Gall a short Passion play
and a Nativity play. The list ends with a fragmentary
Christmas play from Kreuzenstein in the Rhineland,
a Thuringian play of the Wise and Foolish Virgins, a
play of St. Catherine, a play of the Antichrist, and the
so-called Easter play of Maastricht.

It would appear from this survey that before 1400
the harvest of religious drama in both Latin and the
vernacular was thin: the great flowering of such
works came in the fifteenth century, when the mystery play flourished as well.

45. Chambers, *The Med. Stage*, II, p. 74.

Turning now to secular theater,[46] aside from the monologue of Courtois d'Arras, we find the spring play *Jeu de la feuillée*, written about 1262 by Adam de la Hale, also in Arras; he followed this with his pastoral, *Robin et Marion*, about 1283. Like Courtois' text, Rutebeuf's monologue, *Dit de l'herberie*, and the anonymous jest, *L'Enfant et l'Aveugle*, are perhaps not to be reckoned among dramatic productions.

In the fourteenth century we have the four Netherlandish *Abele spelen: Esmoreit, Gloriant, Lanseloet, Vande Winter ende vande Somer*, together with the farces *Lippijn, De Buskenblaser, Die Hexe, Rubben*, and the fragments *Drie Daghe Here* and *Truwanten*. The farces *Nu Noch* and *Playerwater* are from about the same period, as well as the English fragment *Interludium de clerico et puella*, the short Neidhardt farces from Germany, the French *Histoire de Griselidis*, Eustache Deschamps' *Farce de Maître Trubert et d'Antrognart*, and a fragmentary Provençal witch-confession.

These surveys indicate how little parchment was devoted to worldly entertainment; nonetheless this list is scarcely shorter than that of vernacular religious drama for the same period. As for their relative quality, it is obvious that secular drama far excels religious drama in both poetry and dramatic technique. Almost without exception, the religious plays demonstrate lack of structure: unrelated roles are aimlessly thrown in and there is no effort at balance in the scenes. What Church drama, even Greban's great and often poetic Passion mystery written about 1450, can match the

46. It is possible that the Latin works of the twelfth-century Vitalis de Blois, the so-called Plautus-adaptations *Geta* and *Querolus*, just as the *comedia elegiacae*, owe something to the mimes, particularly in their themes, but they were in all probability intended as literary excursions of and for an intellectual group only, and can therefore hardly be included in a list of secular theatrical work.

form and structure of the *Jeu de la feuillée?* How crude and shapeless the mystery plays of the later Middle Ages appear beside the well-constructed tragedy of *Lanseloet.*

This is the more remarkable since secular theater is supposed to have originated from religious drama. Our chronological survey plainly shows that religious drama developed hardly earlier and certainly not further than secular drama. When we also note that in the same period the artistic level of secular drama was much higher than that of religious drama, little reason remains to ascribe a clerical birth to secular theater.

The basis for the art of Adam de la Hale and the poet or poets of the *Abele spelen,* of Rutebeuf and the author of *De Buskenblaser* and *Nu Noch* was the art of the mime, which traditionally upheld from one generation to the next the technique and craftsmanship responsible for the excellence of the first recorded European secular drama. Religious drama completely lacked such background: its authors were clerics, either talented poets like Wipo, who wrote an occasional sublime line, or preachers who wrote to teach. Dramatic training, dramatic thinking, dramatic feeling they lacked utterly; and as we have seen, they turned to the mimes for their performances and for the development of their drama.

But the mimes could never take over complete leadership from the clergy. The plays were written by clerics, who at best, under the mimes' influence, could attempt to adapt their didactic texts to dramatic needs, but who had no real dramatic impulse of their own. We cannot repeat too often that drama is not created merely by the dialogue form; it should not surprise us that clerical dramatic work remained inferior to secular. There is no doubt that the development of the Church theater at the end of the Middle Ages was of great importance for the development of

theater in general, but it lay as little in the nature of
Christianity and within the possibilities of its divine
service to create spontaneously a religious drama as
to cause the rise of a secular theater.

6: The Rites

WHEN A European in the United States is accosted on October 31 by boys and girls in strange costumes and ghostly masks, he cannot be too startled, for he knows such customs from home. He may find it surprising, though, to find that Hallowe'en with its heathen spooks apparently came to the New World on the *Mayflower*, together with its more puritan freight. Hallowe'en is not the only pagan holiday to be translated to America: there is Valentine's Day, on which every boy still chooses his girl in celebration of spring and fertility, just as in Teuton times; there is Yuletide, when songs the lineage of which springs from the *caroles* sung at ancient midwinter feasts resound all over the land.

If neither a distance of thousands of miles nor the strictest Calvinist domination could kill those relics of prehistoric rites, what may we then expect in Europe itself? A great part of its folklore goes straight back to pre-Christian cults and religions, as Grimm and many other historians and ethnologists after him have set forth. That so many ancient customs deriving from heathen ritual still exist, proves that the Germanic tribes did not lightly give up their traditions. Christianization in the seventh and eighth centuries was perforce far from complete. Nowadays these customs are kept up without any understanding of their origin and only for the sake of tradition, but the medieval Church knew quite well where they came from, and for that reason alone could show no tolerance towards them. Nevertheless, the customs lived on, which meant that the conversion was certainly not complete. Paganism, suppressed yet not subdued, merely hid itself under a Christian cloak. This is true above all for the period immediately following the official Christianization of northern Europe. It is exactly at this time that dramatic art reappears.

Aside from some remarks by Roman observers such as Caesar and Tacitus and what may be deduced from the *Edda* and other early collections or writings, our knowledge of Teuton ritual is mainly based on reconstructions emanating from the folk customs as they are found and described in later times. They indicate —as we might well expect—that the same circumstances as in other archaic civilizations prevailed in Europe and led to the same world-conception and the same kind of ritual. Just as in the rest of the world, primitive man in Europe depended upon the succession of the seasons; deviations in nature's periodicity immediately put him in peril of death. He too longed for the return of summer and fertility; he too did his best to compel the ruling forces, by charms and by dances, to conform to his desires.

In general, reconstruction from relics of prehistoric civilization is a highly risky business, the more so as each interpretation usually turns for its originator into an unquestionable dogma. Dissension naturally results —how much dissension is there, for instance, in such a relatively simple matter as that of the antique theater building, of which literary and observable material is still abundant.[1] In the case of the Germanic ritual only customs are left, and even the origin of those of which the derivation seems clear and definite may suddenly be challenged and drawn into dispute.[2] Es-

1. Cf. B. Hunningher, *Acoustics and Acting in the Theatre of Dionysus Eleuthereus,* Meded. Kon. Akademie v. Wetensch. afd. lett., 1956, Amsterdam; especially notes 1 and 3.
2. Karl Meissen, *Nikolauskult und Nikolausbrauch im Abendlande, Forschungen zur Volkskunde,* Düsseldorf, 1931, denies all pagan influence.

pecially since the many prewar German publications, boldly and without ado, deduced most of West European folklore and culture entirely from the pure, high civilization of the Teuton tribes,[3] we must take special care to observe Jan de Vries' warning:[4] "We should not perceive in every strawdoll a vegetation-spirit, we should not regard every pageant as an ancient heathen ritual act, nor should we interpret every figure baked in bread as a sacrifice-substitute."

From the vast evidence of these pagan survivals, we choose one of most outspoken character, the so-called *Perhtenlauf*, which still prevails in parts of the Alps, especially in the Tirol valleys and the Salzburg neighborhood. During the ritually important period from Christmas until Twelfth Night, young men wearing masks of terrifying aspect, clad in sheep- and badgerskins, with bell-girdles around their waists, dance and run with great uproar through town and field. Often there are special types among them with less frightening features: the drummer, the fool and his girl, a boy in women's clothes, and particularly the quack. They may break into houses and annoy the inmates, or they may only pass, yelling and dancing, till suddenly the wild Perht appears among them: the Unknown One. Then they break into an ecstatic, breath-taking dance, and in growing frenzy they jump higher and higher, finally trying to spring over the well-beam: in water dwell the unseen forces. Sometimes, however, the mummers rush in fear to the nearest house, for under a rooftree they are safe from the wild Perht; at other times they chase the man with the devil's mask and slay him. In Salzburg several isolated stone crosses still indicate the places where such victims were buried; for whoever died wearing the

3. Otto Höfler, *Kultische Geheimbünde der Germanen*, Frankfurt a.M., 1934. Richard Wolfram, *Schwerttänze und Männerbund*, Kassel, 1936. Robert Stumpfl, *Kultspiele der Germanen*—
4. Jan de Vries, *Altgermanische Religionsgeschichte*, 1 (Grundr. der Germ. Philologie), p. 305.

devil's mask was not admitted to a Christian cemetery. From its very beginning, the Church has identified all the daemons of paganism with the devil and consigned them as demons to hell.

The daemon celebrated in this rite, the ecstasy of which seems very close to the Dionysiac mania, was Perhta, a figure related to Frau Holle and imagined as an old woman leading a train of wandering souls, especially those of dead children. "The Perhtenlauf is a rite of movement, connected with the mimic presentation of the train of roaming souls, to stimulate the animalistic and vegetative fertility," as Waschnitius put it, in his study of the custom.[5] He took occasion to demonstrate how here, too, the mimic presentation of the daemons aims at overpowering the other-worldly force and at acquiring through ecstasy super-human qualities for the participants in the rite. In Gastein the story is still told of the boy who, on the advice of an old woman, did not read his prayers for fourteen days and then in springing over the well at the *Perhtenlauf* remained floating in the air; the priest's exorcism brought him down wailing, and, full of praise for the ecstasy of his flight, he died.

This European custom brings us straightway back to the primitive and archaic rites we discussed earlier. The *Perhtenlauf* not only reminds us of the Maenads' wild fury, it shows also such features as group dance, communal ecstasy, imitative presentation through masks of other-worldly forces as we found character-istic of all pagan ritual. Just as among primitives, the Gastein boy's bliss was no heavenly gift, but an achievement of his own. The slaying of the daemon-

5. Viktor Waschnitius, *Perht, Holda und verwandte Gestalten. Beitrag zur Deutschen Religionsgeschichte.* Sitz. ber. d. Kais. Ak. d. Wissensch, in Wien, Phil.-Hist. Kl. 174 Band, 2 Abh. "Er ist ein Bewegungsritus, verbunden mit einer mimischen Darstellung des umziehenden Seelenheeres zur Förderung der animalischen und vegetabilen Fruchtbarkeit." (p. 159) For Gastein boy: p. 58.

performer, the presence of the quack or medicine man might lead to further conclusions were it not for de Vries' pertinent warning. Only this should be added: the *Perhtenlauf* itself has been observed exclusively during the winter solstice, though closely related to it is a similar processional dance, the *Streggelejagen*, customarily performed in the nights around Easter near Lucerne.

Easter brought the morris dance[6] to England as well as to the Continent, also a procession of disguised dancers with blackened faces, the "Moors" from whom the custom derived its name. Here also the participants wore dresses and belts with bells, and again dancers of special types joined the procession: the fool in a horrid mask, the man in women's dress, the friar and—especially in England—the hobbyhorse. These personages clearly reflect imitative action and mimic performance. Wild behavior suited such participants, who carried staves and wooden swords and often caused turbulent situations. Such a show of weapons suggests that these processions were influenced by the sword dances described by Tacitus as a Germanic rite and still known, especially in the Alps region, under different forms and names—for instance, the so-called *Rapper-tanz.*[7]

Eastertide and Christmastide were also the periods when dance processions were most frequent in the medieval Church. On Christmas Night of the year 1020 the priest in the church of Kölbigk near Anhalt[8] was about to celebrate the Mass, when a wild group of men and women broke into the sacred building itself and danced there frenetically, singing their unholy *cantica obscoena, diabolica.* Neither the objurgations of the priest nor the efforts of his assistants could stop

6. See Chambers, *The Med. Stage,* I, p. 195 note.
7. See Wolfram, *op. cit.*
8. See A. Tille, *Die Geschichte der deutschen Weihnacht,* Leipzig, 1832, p. 301.

them, until heaven stepped in and killed several, putting the rest to flight. They struggled for a year as lunatics in the woods and fields before the priest would lift the curse from them.

This story was widespread in the Middle Ages; it indicates the Church's hatred of these pagan relics and proves the error of attributing the origin of such dance-processions to the Church itself.[9] Gougaud[10] has gathered a thorny bouquet of Council decrees from the years 589 to 1617, fierce attacks on this custom which certainly leave no place for the slightest doubt in the matter: there could never be any question of admitting sacred dances into the liturgy of the Church. "Elle n'a favorisé ni encouragé l'introduction de la danse dans les églises," Gougaud says.

From the beginning the Church rightly saw in this custom its ritual origin and stigmatized it as heresy. Chrysostom[11] as well as Augustine[12] frowned upon the Jewish sabbath dance: *melius enim utique tota die foderent, quam tota die saltarent*—better to dig than to dance. But these dances can hardly be Jewish in origin. In spite of all bans against them they managed to intrude into the Church in many places. The fight was the fiercer since these dances were objectionable not only as pagan relics, but also from their open references to fertility, often leading to obscene expressions and forms. This sharply clashed with the morality imposed by the Church.

Best known of all dances in the Church is the *carole*, a ring-dance about which Caesarius of Arles complained as early as the middle of the sixth century. It was danced without instrumental accompaniment,

9. Andreas Heusler, *Deutsche Versgeschichte*, I, Berlin, 1925, p. 20.
10. L. Gougaud, "La danse dans les églises," *Revue d'histoire ecclésiastique*, XV, Louvain, 1914, p. 5 and p. 229 seq.
11. J. P. Migne, *P.G.*, XLVIII, p. 845.
12. J. P. Migne, *P.L.*, XXXVIII, p. 77.

but, just as among primitive tribes, the rhythm was indicated by clapping of hands and stamping of feet, while all kinds of secular songs were sung. It certainly is not "fatalément," as Gougaud thinks, but remarkable that when in his *Gemma Animae* Honorius of Autun intended to describe the dances of the pagans before their idols, he simply set forth the profane dances of his own time. His interpretation of the movements may be unacceptable to us, but his description clearly proves the mimetic character of these dances. In his *Constitutio de abolendis reliquiis idolatriae* at the end of the sixth century the Merovingian Childebert II banned all dances at Easter and Christmas—as we know, with little result. That the Church itself openly recognized the parallel between Christian Easter and the old festival for the return of summer is plain in such hymns as *Salve festa dies*, still sung at the Easter procession in many a church:

> *Ecce renascentis testatur gratia mundi*
> *Omnia cum Domino dona redisse suo.*
> *Namque triumphanti post tristia tartara Christo*
> *Undique fronde nemus, gramina flore favent.*[13]

Emile Mâle conjectured[14] that the late medieval dances of death reflected performances observed by the painters and designers. This is certainly quite possible, inasmuch as such presentations may be linked with those dance processions on cemeteries condemned by several Council decrees, quoted by Gougaud. It is not Christendom, but paganism that believes in a continuing community of the quick and the dead, it is paganism that involves the ancestors, always part of

13. "See the grace of the reborn earth proves that all gifts have come back with their Lord. For when Christ returns triumphant from the gloom of Hell then everywhere the woods please him with foliage, the fields with flowers."
14. Emile Mâle, *L'Art à la fin du moyen âge,* Paris, 1908, p. 391. See also Curt Sachs, *op. cit.,* p. 252.

the tribe, in its cults and festivals. That, by the way, these dances of death were of mimic character is more than evident from the drawings and prints of them.

Extremely interesting, of course, are those church dances in which the clergy itself participated. Most of them belong again to the celebration of Christmas and Easter. As early as 911, these *tripudia* (dances in three-step) are mentioned as they were performed right in the famous monastery of St. Gall from which the trope sprang. Connected with these dances are the Feasts of All Fools, of which the later Middle Ages have so much to tell, and also the Rule of the Boy-Bishop.[15] "Priests and clergy may be seen wearing masks and monstrous visages at the hours of office. They dance in the choir dressed as women, panders or minstrels," as at such a Feast of Fools in 1445. The element of mimic imitation was even stronger in the farce of the boy-bishop.

The same cannot be said of such performances as the Easter dance in Auxerre,[16] where the clergy danced in the nave singing the *Victimae paschali laudes* and throwing balls, or of such still existing church dances as the *Spring-Procession* in Echternach or the *Seizes* in Seville. All of them were extremely hard to exterminate, if they were exterminable at all.

This list of customs and dances might lead to far-reaching inferences, especially as so many details—such as the slaying of the daemon, the appearance of such possible relatives of the old medicine man as quack and friar, the communal ecstasy and the use of masks—induce us to draw parallels with primitive rites. From these data, however, it is clear and irrefutable that in the early period of Christianity in Western Europe the periods of Easter and Christmas

15. See Chambers, *The Med. Stage*, I, p. 274, 336.
16. See Gougaud, *loc. cit.*

were distinguished by much dancing, which, as in all
folk dances, showed a highly mimetic and imitative
character. From what could they have inherited such
essential features but from the ritual dance?

We could, however, refuse to accept the fact that
ritual dance existed among the Celts and Teutons during the Winter and Spring Festival.[17] Where then did
these processions and dances come from? In its essence and character Christianity itself could never
have given birth to these phenomena, in which the
medieval Church recognized the symptoms of heresy.
Did it then, in spite of itself, serve unknowingly and
unwillingly as the channel through which these dances
penetrated from the Mediterranean region into the
North? [18] We found, however, as many dance customs
outside as inside the Church. Furthermore, such un-
awareness on the part of the Church in transferring
customs it deeply disliked, is hardly acceptable, even
though it is a fact that now and then it has taken over
heathen customs, after due Christianization, into the
official liturgy.

In that very incorporation, the Church showed
from the beginning how extremely well aware it was
of the danger from paganism and its thousand-year-
old traditions. It scored a great success by introducing
its adoption policy, which in itself proves how little
the Church can be conceived of as unaware of what
it did. It was further protected: however tolerant
the local clergy might be, the Holy See itself remained
very strict, so that official adoption could follow only

17. Chambers, *The Med. Stage*, I, p. 228, rejects a winter
solstice festival with the Germanic tribes; disputed by A. F.
Feilberg, *Jul*, Kopenhagen, 1904 and M. Nilsson, *Studien zur
Vorgeschichte des Weihnachtsfestes*, Arch. für Religionswis-
sensch. XIX, p. 50 seq.
18. A. Heusler, *Die Altgermanische Dichtung* (Handbuch der.
Lit. Wissensch.), Potsdam, 1929, p. 43; "Es gab genug rö-
misches, mittelmeerisches Heidentum, das unter dem Krumstab
fortwucherte."

after sharp examination and long consideration. The case of the trope proves this.

Gregory the Great[19] under whom the Christianization of Europe was so energetically undertaken, formulated and introduced this adoption policy. His words are famous—"the Holy Church corrects things through its fervor, tolerates others in mansuetude, dissimulates and bears some out of consideration—*ut saepe malum quod aversatur, portando et dissimulando compescat*": by toleration and dissimulation evil may be curbed. The missionaries and later the clergy in Western Europe faithfully followed these words, and Gregory's wise policy certainly facilitated the transition of its habitants from paganism to Christianity. For posterity, however, it blurred the distinctions, with the result that we will never know from which tradition actions originated, which are by now venerated customs.

Outside the Church, of course, folklore of the winter festival and the springtime abounds; and though most of it has acquired a sacred veneer, we are in no doubt about the heathen beginnings. Inside the Church the situation is more complicated: it is highly probable, for instance, that in the fourth century Christ's birthday[20] was fixed on December 25th in order to usurp the heathen sun festival, *Natalis Invicti*. But this can never be proved. Of the consecration of fires on Holy Saturday Eisenhofer[21] states: "they were in all probability introduced to suppress the heathen Germanic fire of spring." It is the same with every procession, every saint's day, every sacred or venerated place. However obvious their pagan origin may seem to be, they are by now all hallowed by the Church and at

19. J. P. Migne, *P.L.*, LXXVII, p. 1191.
20. A. Meyer, *Das Weihnachtsfest, seine Erstehung und Entwicklung*, Tübingen, 1913.
21. Ludwig Eisenhofer, *Handbuch der Katholischen Liturgik*, Freiburg i.B., 1932, p. 535.

any time they can be claimed to be pure Christian institutions—as for instance, E. Meissen did for St. Nicholas and his festival. In fact the situation we face in Europe is somewhat similar to the one in Greece described by Jane Harrison:[22] there art absorbed ritual; here it was another ritual, the liturgy of the Church in its official and unofficial forms that absorbed the heathen rites. As a result, from here on we can progress only over the thin ice of supposition; for some it may seem much thicker than others, for religious reasons, will ever acknowledge.

That pre-Christian Europe, like the entire primitive world, celebrated the return of light and of summer is evident from the innumerable customs still in existence. The Maypoles, the Easter dances, the feasting of Twelfth Night, the Christmas bonfires and many other traditions all testify to this. Since the missionaries found the population naturally much attached to the old ritual honoring the victory of summer over winter, why should they not have facilitated conversion by adopting along the official lines what could be taken over without doing active harm?

E. K. Chambers[23] thinks that the power of heathenism at that time should not be overrated; at the introduction of Christianity "the worshippers of the Keltic and Teutonic deities already practised a traditional ritual, probably without any clear conception of the *rationale* on which some at least of the acts which they performed were based." However, the strength and stamina of customs and of ritual above all, do not depend on the definite and intelligible significance for the worshippers. What supports them is fear as well as fun: these two elements maintain above the level of logic and reason most of the traditions in modern civilization; it was such elements that gave pagan ritual

22. Jane E. Harrison, *Ancient Art and Ritual*, p. 14.
23. Chambers, *The Med. Stage*, I, p. 99.

and customs the tenacity that forced the Church to its policy of adoption.

This makes clear why such strange dances as we mentioned before could survive, why some of them could penetrate even into the churches. Or had they been performed on these spots long before the churches existed, before the buildings were converted from heathen into Christian use? In any case, we found that they were performed especially at the Easter and Christmas periods and we defined most of them as mimetic and imitative in character.

In an earlier chapter we saw that among primitive men such dances sprang from the desire for the return of summer and from joy at its reappearance. But save for some vague exceptions on isolated spots where these dances do not seem to exist, this is the general pattern over the whole archaic world.[24] What reason can there be to assume that the many races and peoples that lived through the ages in Europe before the advent of Christianity formed an exception to this pattern? What is there to prove definitively that they in their dances, of which we have so many relics, did not express their desire for the return of fertility and their happiness over spring's arrival? As the situation of primitive men in Europe was the same as everywhere else and as not the slightest evidence exists of a different evolution there, these circumstances must have produced the same results as elsewhere.

The possibility of exception always remains, however. Though a speaking likeness may exist between the customs in Europe which we mentioned and the primitive rites which produced cult-drama, that likeness in itself is not sufficient to make us simply accept as a fact that archaic rites in Europe and in the rest of the world were the same and for that reason a

24. K. Pearson, *The Chances of Death and Other Studies in Evolution*, London-New York, 1897, II, p. 280.

ritual drama must have existed there before the introduction of Christianity. Material evidence of such
drama in remnants or relics simply does not exist.

This fact, of course, is well known; otherwise historians of modern drama never would have indulged in
all the guesses and theories we have summed up before. Yet some of them did not direct their inquiries
into the period preceding the reappearance of written
drama but found a solution in trope and liturgy. Later,
some exploration of pre-Christian relics was undertaken: though no direct remainders of drama were
found, there was always the possibility that other
monuments of archaic European culture would testify
indirectly about the state of drama.

Apparently inspired by Gilbert Murray's investiga-
tions into the origin of Greek drama, Bertha S. Phillpotts[25] searched the *Elder Edda* thoroughly and found
ample evidence and indication of theater, of ritual
marriage, and fertility drama. Her study is of great
interest and importance for those who accept her
hypothesis that many parts of the Scandinavian epic
are clear and coherent only if seen as remnants of the
religious drama which they reflect, at that time familiar
to the entire Teutonic world. Such scholars certainly
will answer in the affirmative the author's final question: "Was not the real cause of the inclusion of
drama in the liturgy the fact that to the mass of converts of the Teutonic peoples religion was so inti-
mately connected with dramatic representations that
the Teutonic priest sought drama in the Christian
liturgy and introduced it where he could, in response
to an overwhelming demand, which he himself probably shared to some extent?" But for those who cannot
accept Miss Phillpotts' theory, her solution as well as
her question must remain basically negligible.

This situation repeats itself more or less in Vilhelm

25. Bertha S. Phillpotts, *The Elder Edda*—cf. page 24, note 22.

Grønbeck's extensive discussion of ritual drama in his *Culture of the Teutons*.[26] After demonstrating the dramatic quality in the religion of the old Europeans, he particularly analyzed the *Vøluspa*, a stanzaic poem from the Viking period. Outwardly, the poem appears to have been influenced by the apocalyptic prophecies of the Church, but in fact it is deeply rooted in conceptions of old Germanic religion which it exclusively reflects. For Grønbeck, the references to dramatic performances in the poem are clear and striking. Similarly clear are indications of the theater in a group of *Edda*-songs, related to the story of Sigurd's victory over the dragon.

From the Hebrew Asif, from Perseus up to St. George, the fight of hero and dragon is unquestionably an image and myth of summer's battle and triumph over winter performed in ritual. Not every story of a similar fight, however, is in itself necessarily a cogent mark of drama. This evidence will never persuade, for instance, adherents of other theories. As a matter of fact, only script-fragments of pagan drama could achieve that. As long as they are not found, we may as well transfer our attention to later times.

In many liturgical plays worldly scenes appear, so prominent in the performance that some see in these *intermezzi* the real source of secular drama.[27] As may be concluded from the preceding paragraphs I incline to ascribe the growth of such scenes as that of the unguent merchant who comically attends the three Marys to the influence of the mimes; others may find their solutions elsewhere. Most interesting in this respect are the endeavors of Robert Stumpfl: with considerable speculation, he attempts to show[28]

26. Vilhelm Grønbeck, *The Culture of the Teutons*—cf. page 24, note 22.
27. Alfred Bäschlin, *Die altdeutsche Salberkrämerspiele,* diss. Basel, 1929.
28. Robert Stumpfl, *op. cit.,* p. 222 seq.; cf. A. Nicoll, *op. cit.,* p. 186.

the heathen roots of this widespread and much-loved burlesque, so sharply contrasting with the surrounding scenes in the Easter plays.

His suspicions were aroused by the fact that in the German plays the name *Mercator* is nearly always accompanied by the word *Medicus*. This, together with the fact that in the Czech quack-play *Mastičkar*, the Mercator announces his power to resurrect the dead and then indeed revives a boy, are Stumpfl's main reasons for regarding this Mercator-Medicus as related to the medicine man of ritual drama, whose task it was to revive the slain figure of winter. In the Mercator's wife, and especially in his servant Ruprecht, he finds other ties with pre-Christian times, while he relates the regular appearance of the three Marys to the veneration of three matrons as givers of fertility, to which several carved stones testify.[29] The Herod-*intermezzi* in the Christmas plays, which shocked Herrad of Landsburg because of their unholy and coarse character, are traced by Stumpfl to the pagan rites of initiation into the tribes. Whether one should ascribe so many and such long-lasting influences to his "extatische Männerbünde" seems doubtful. That in both *intermezzi* remnants of dramatic rite can be found is, however, highly probable.[30]

With these interludes we come nearer to the secular plays extant in manuscript, the themes of which tie them inseparably to the combat of winter and summer, to the succession of death and resurrection. The thirteenth-century French *Jeu de la feuillée* and the fourteenth-century Netherlandish *Abel spel vande Winter ende vande Somer* are based on the fight of the

29. J. de Vries, "Studiën over Germaanse Mythologie," *Tijdschrift*, Leiden, 1931, p. 112.
30. For other theatrical customs which are less important for the develoment see Maximilian J. Rudwin, *The Origin of the German Carnival Comedy*—cf. p. 8, note 1, and Samuel L. Sumberg, *The Nüremberg Schembart Carnival*, diss. Columbia Un., 1941.

seasons and the victory of summer. They certainly do not both belong to the category of folk plays, and Chambers' comment on the English *Robin Hood* plays and the *Jeu de Robin et Marion* holds true for them: "they were written not by the folk themselves, but by *trouvères* or minstrels for the folk."

This was, in fact, just the same way as that in which Euripides wrote his *Bacchai* for the Athenians. Like the Greek tragedian, the *trouvères* drew from popular traditions that lived among and in the people. To suggest, as has been done, that these poets wished to be independent and original even in theme[31] and motive results from typically modern conceptions. That separately and independently Adam le Bossu and the author of the Netherlandish play took as a theme the combat of winter and summer proves considerably more than the mere fact that the combat was still known in twelfth- and thirteenth-century Europe. The material on village festivals and other folklore, gathered by Chambers and others,[32] has made that clear. What is even more significant, however, is that in the early period of West European vernacular literature, this combat is not first described in prose or in epic poetry,[33] but is twice reflected precisely in dramatic form. It is more than likely that both *trouvères* knew that combat in its dramatic form and used what they had seen as material for their literary works.

These plays provide us with enough evidence to accept the theory that the rules of primitive society worked in Europe as in the rest of the world, and the

31. Chambers' remarks in *The Med. Stage*, I, p. 182 that this happened "at a period when the independent evolution of the religious play had already set a model of dramatic composition" is, as our chronological survey showed, at least highly exaggerated.

32. Cf. Frazer, *op. cit.*, I, p. 98 seq.

33. This does not contradict the theory that many epic poems reflect this theme indirectly.

same circumstances produced the same results for drama. For we cannot assume that a winter-summer play produced about the year 1200 in Europe had no Continental pedigree but that the theme had been imported from some other more primitive parts of the world.

In connection with the Mummers' play Chambers[34] has given some consideration to the *St. George* plays, which at the end of the Middle Ages were well known in England and on the Continent; in the middle of the sixteenth century Pieter Breughel depicted one of them, the *Kermis van Sint Jeroen*, and in several regions these plays are still performed. Though Chambers does not deny the possibility that the struggle of the champions goes back to the contest of summer and winter, he detaches himself quickly enough from this idea and from the whole subject.

Arthur Beatty[35] has taken up the research on this topic and the results of his far deeper study are impressive: he found that most such performances have common features. Among the most striking are the drawing of a circle, inside which the players stand when playing their parts; a fight between individuals, or a melée; the death and revival of one or more persons accomplished by a bragging Doctor. "Taking the Lutterworth play as the norm, Prince George fights the Turkish knight and is mortally wounded. The Doctor comes in and revives the Prince." In comparing the legends about the Saint with these plays Beatty pointed out: "According to the church legend, St. George does not marry the rescued maiden. In-

34. Chambers, *The Med. Stage,* I, p. 218 seq. and II, p. 276. In his *English Folk-play,* Oxford, 1933, p. 210 and 216 he sees more connection between year-drama and mummers-play.
35. Arthur Beatty, *The St. George, or Mummers' Plays: a study in the protology of drama.* Transactions of the Wisconsin Ac. of Science, Arts and Letters, XV, part II, 1907, p. 293.

stead he gives the would-be father-in-law some sound orthodox advice and leaves. But in the Lutterworth play St. George proclaims:

> *I slew the fiery dragon and brought him to the slaughter,*
> *And won the King of Egypt's only daughter.*"

So far as the Doctor is concerned, it is certainly most interesting that the speech he yells out in some of the folk plays is nearly identical with the speech of the Mercator in a twelfth-century Easter Play from Tours, in a thirteenth-century play called *Les trois Maries*, in the Alsfelder Passion Play from twelfth-century Germany, and other scenes of the unguent merchant. As is quite plain, this coincides extremely well with Stumpfl's Doctor-Mercator theory.

Even if we assume that the St. George play, with all its incident and detail, springs from the regular liturgical drama, we are left with some difficulty, as Beatty has shown. In the first place, in the legends the Saint always fights and conquers a dragon or monster,[36] but he himself is never killed. In the plays, on the other hand, he is killed as often as he conquers. In the second place, the one constant and central incident of the St. George plays is the revival of all the persons who were killed. In the liturgical plays, however, the dead stay dead, while in the St. George plays there does not "seem to be any idea of such an outcome."

These findings do more than fit in well with some of our preceding evidence: they formidably fortify the theory that ritual drama was as well known among the pre-Christian Europeans as among primitive civilizations elsewhere. Though no written traces of it may be left, its relics in folk customs of later centuries are so persistent and manifest that they prove the existence

36. In the Netherlandish St. George play the dragon is not killed but tamed. See P. Leendertz, *Middelned. Dram. Poëzie,* p. 432.

of that drama before and its continuation during and after the Christianization of Europe. It was certainly in a position to make its influence felt on the new drama at that time growing inside and outside the Church.

We must stress once more that ritual drama everywhere centers on the burial of winter and the resurrection of life; once more we must remember that the first liturgical drama is found just at Easter. Before long, however, Christmas plays were mentioned within the Church and, as we know from Gougaud, Easter and Christmas were also the periods in which the pagan dance-mania regularly manifested itself both around and in the churches.

From the raging of the Maenads to the Western *Perhtenlauf* many of these dances were performed in the dark. We hear of bonfires at Easter and Christmas, of torchlight processions through the fields at the solstice of winter, the vernal equinox, and the night of May 1. Hallowe'en and other traditional customs do not get under way until after sunset. The German *Weihnachten* and *Fastnacht* as well as the English *Twelfth Night* testify how important the night, and especially the night before a festival, has always been in Europe's folklore.[37] It was during the night that the dancers of Kölbigk broke into the church, and according to the Council of Avignon,[38] in 1209, many ecclesiastic vigils were disturbed by the wild singing and dancing of similar groups. In the dark the material existence of man faded out; it was the proper time for many of his ecstatic pagan rites, to which sunrise brought an end.

In view of the Church's adoption policy it is not surprising to learn that during the eves and nights

37. See Frazer, *op. cit.*, ch. LXII and Mannhardt, *Wald- und Feldkulte*, I, p. 497 seq.
38. J. D. Mansi, *Sacrorum Conciliorum et Decretorum Nova et Amplissima Collectio*, Florence, 1759, XXII, p. 791 seq.

of saints' days vigils and services were held in honor
of the martyr of that day and that often such exercises
were emphasized with ecclesiastic splendor. The
Church knew how tenacious a competitor paganism
was, how hard to subdue; this is proved by the fact
that in these *laetitia* disorderly dancing, profane singing, and feasting were often observable. Again, such
disturbances took place chiefly on the Eve and Night
of both Easter and Christmas. Albeit reluctantly, they
were tolerated: it is quite probable that the Kölbigk
dancers were surprised by the harsh punishment that
suddenly fell upon them.

It is clear now that even in the eleventh and twelfth
centuries, in several spots in Western Europe the night
before Easter was dedicated to dancing and revelry
which originated in pagan customs connected with
such fertility rites as the burial and the resurrection of
the year-drama. When such debauchery could maintain itself through several centuries of Christian rule,
how powerful and violent its forms of appearance
must have been in the period of Christianization,
which lasted at least till the ninth century. Such ob-
stacles to the Church could only be overcome by
adoption: why should the Church not fight its competitor on his own ground? In celebrating Christ's
resurrection at Easter why should it not meet the
pagan or the nearly converted halfway and appropriate
his rites, which celebrated a resurrection too, and,
what is more, even represented it? The fight with
heathenism was fierce and vehement. From ancient
times that ritual had been built up to a form that
certainly must have come very close to perfection.
How was it possible for missionaries and priests to
compete with such acts and performances? Help and
rescue could come only from the professional actors
and performers—the mimes.

If we accept such a course of events, then the birth
scene of modern drama seems to acquire more light

and coherence: cause and effect at last harmonize. For now there is an urge compelling Christendom to representation, to acting and drama, in spite of its entirely untheatrical essence and character. If the word alone could not win, then the act would be a powerful ally. So it happened that theater was not reborn in the Church, but was adopted and taken in by her, however great the distance originally had been that separated this unworldly faith from the love of world and worldly life, out of which all theater sprang.

But then it was not a change in the liturgical order which generated drama, as K. Young said. Hymns like the tropes which in question and answer were alternately sung by sections of the choir, did not turn into drama simply because they were given opportunity to expand. When they are brought together with real and living theater, however—are grafted upon this new stock, so to speak—then all kinds of new possibilities come into being. So we may assume that the Easter trope was not transferred to the end of the Matins for reasons of space alone, but to make it coincide with those pagan rites performed on the eve and night of the spring festival, in order to Christianize those heathen vigils and exercises by means of holy dialogue. Aside from competition, there was every reason to bring them together, as in both elements, Christian and pagan, the main theme consisted of a burial followed by the triumph and glory of the resurrection.

Such a development certainly makes the rise of drama in the Church's liturgy entirely understandable: now it finds a natural breeding-ground from which it can draw its strength for further growth. Does not its genesis in pagan drama also account for the fact that the liturgical Easter play concentrated for some time upon burial and resurrection, and not until the thirteenth century extended itself to the sufferings and passion of Christ?

All this is conjecture, of course. The fact that all pieces seem to fit well now does not prove that we have succeeded in reconstructing the original sequence of events. All the same, we did not jump to our conclusions and the indications, the symptoms, and parallels that seem to justify the proposal of such construction are many.

We called up the theater and listened to its testimony. In refining its essence from the variety of forms in which it has appeared, we found out what belongs to the possibilities of theater and what is utterly foreign to it. Its own standard forms the only certainty in the maze of problems and enigmas that surround its origin.

But not all judges will accept this certainty, for however strange it may seem, there are still many workers in the field of drama who have and want no contact with the living theater. It must sound strange to them that Gustave Cohen, at the end of a long life filled with scholarly research and publications, could appraise his collaboration with his students in re-enacting and so resurrecting the medieval theater as "the most valuable and most durable" of all his accomplishments.[39] However, their suspicion and challenging of the theater's testimony should not be disregarded; the problems are too intricate and the ground too slippery not to heed each and every warning.

We do not claim more for our proposal than Léon Gautier did for his solution; both lack the material evidence necessary to irrefutable establishment. "I dare not say *the* origin—and yet I am tempted to believe it is," he said. Such testimony does not provide certainty either, and clearly is not intended to do so. Gautier can not be blamed because his hypothesis was later taken for solid fact and used as the basis of the

39. Gustave Cohen, *Etudes d'histoire du théâtre en France au moyen age et à la rénaissance* (Paris, 1956), pp. 10 and 441.

belief that the theater rose out of the Church's liturgy. We follow him in his hopes and doubts when we re-place his *trope* with our *pagan rites*. I can't quite say that it is *the* origin, and yet I am tempted to believe that it is.

Index

DRAMABOOKS

CRITICISM